Always Movin' On

OTHER BOOKS BY JAMES S. HASKINS

Diary of a Harlem Schoolteacher
Resistance: Profiles in Nonviolence
Revolutionaries: Agents of Change
The War and the Protest: Vietnam
Profiles in Black Power
A Piece of the Power: Four Black Mayors
From Lew Alcindor to Kareem Abdul Jabbar
Black Manifesto for Education (Editor)
Religions
The Psychology of Black Language
  with Hugh F. Butts, M.D.
Jokes from Black Folks
Pinckney Benton Stewart Pinchback
Ralph Bunche: A Most Reluctant Hero
Adam Clayton Powell: Portrait of a Marching Black
Witchcraft, Mysticism and Magic in the Black World
Street Gangs: Yesterday and Today
Babe Ruth and Hank Aaron: The Home Run Kings
Snow Sculpture and Ice Carving: The Art of Creating Transient Forms
The Consumer Movement
The Picture Life of Malcolm X
Fighting Shirley Chisholm
The Creoles of Color of New Orleans
Dr. J: A Biography of Julius Erving
Your Rights: Past and Present
The Story of Stevie Wonder

Always Movin' On

THE LIFE OF LANGSTON HUGHES

by James S. Haskins

FRANKLIN WATTS
New York/London/1976

I am grateful to my editors for their help with this book, to Mary Ellen Arrington, who typed the manuscript drafts, and to Kathy Benson, without whom this book would not have been possible.

Photographs courtesy of:
Countee Cullen Papers, Amistad Research Center: p. 23; National Association for the Advancement of Colored People: p. 26; National Archives: Harmon Foundation Collection: p. 30, U.S. Information Agency: p. 90; Moorland-Springarn Research Center, Howard University: The Rose McClendon Memorial Collection of Photographs of Celebrated Negroes by Carl Van Vechten, p. 37, The Mary O'H. Williamson Collection, p. 86; United Press International: pp. 42, 68, 105; The Bettmann Archive: pp. 46, 58; Library of Congress: p. 62.

Library of Congress Cataloging in Publication Data

Haskins, James, 1941–
Always movin' on.

Bibliography: p.
Includes index.
SUMMARY: A biography of Langston Hughes, an Afro-American poet who tried to capture in his writing the spirit and rhythms of ordinary people.
1. Hughes, Langston, 1902–1967—Biography—Juvenile literature. [1. Hughes, Langston, 1902–1967. 2. Poets, American 3. Afro-Americans—Biography] I. Title.
PS3515.U274Z656 818'.5'209 [B] 76–16107
ISBN 0–531–01211–5

Printed in the United States of America
5 4 3

Acknowledgments

Selections from *The Best of Simple,* © 1961 by Langston Hughes, reprinted by permission of Farrar, Straus & Giroux, Inc.

Selections from *The Big Sea,* © 1963 by Langston Hughes, reprinted by permission of Farrar, Straus & Giroux, Inc.

Selections from *I Wonder As I Wander,* © 1956 by Langston Hughes, reprinted by permission of Farrar, Straus & Giroux, Inc.

Lines from "The Backlash Blues" from *The Panther and the Lash: Poems of Our Times,* by Langston Hughes, copyright © 1967 by Arna Bontemps and George Houston Bass. Reprinted by permission of Alfred A. Knopf, Inc., and Harold Ober Associates Incorporated.

"Reasons Why" copyright 1932 by Alfred A. Knopf, Inc., and renewed 1960 by Langston Hughes. Reprinted from *The Dream Keeper and Other Poems,* by Langston Hughes, by permission of Alfred A. Knopf, Inc.

"The Negro Speaks of Rivers" copyright 1926 by Alfred A. Knopf, Inc., and renewed 1954 by Langston Hughes; "When Sue Wears Red" copyright 1926 by Alfred A. Knopf, Inc., and renewed 1954 by Langston Hughes; lines from "The Weary Blues" copyright 1926 by Alfred A. Knopf, Inc., and renewed 1954 by Langston Hughes; "Madam's Past History" copyright 1948 by Alfred A. Knopf, Inc.; lines from "Wake" copyright 1942 and renewed 1970 by Arna Bontemps and George Houston Bass: reprinted from *Selected Poems,* by Langston Hughes, by permission of the publisher.

Lines from "International Brigades, Somewhere in Spain, 1937" published in *I Wonder As I Wander*, copyright 1956 by Langston Hughes, reprinted by permission of Harold Ober Associates Incorporated.

"The Mills" published in *The Big Sea*, copyright 1940 by Alfred A. Knopf, Inc., Renewed. Reprinted by permission of Harold Ober Associates Incorporated.

"Love is Like the Breath of a Rose" published in *The Big Sea*, copyright 1940 by Alfred A. Knopf, Inc., Renewed. Reprinted by permission of Harold Ober Associates Incorporated.

Contents

Introduction

In a career spanning some forty-five years, Langston Hughes made a large and unique contribution not only to American literature but to black American cultural life and to American humor as well. Though he began his writing career as a poet, he also became successful as a novelist, a reporter, a translator, a playwright, and a short-story writer. The body of his work includes thirty-nine volumes of his own, four full-length translated works, sixty-six published short stories, numerous plays, and hundreds of uncollected pieces. But more important than numbers is the kind of work he produced.

In a time when many other black poets were writing poems that were no different from those of white poets, and when some black prose writers were writing only about well-to-do, educated blacks, Langston chose not only to write about poor, uneducated blacks, but to write about them with the spirit and rhythms of jazz and the blues, the music of ordinary black people.

There is a lot of pain and sadness in the lives of the people in Langston Hughes' poems and stories, just as there was much pain and sadness in his own life. The product of an unsettled and insecure childhood, black in a white society, despite his fame he never achieved contentment. Yet his was not really an unhappy life, for he was able to look at it with a sense of humor, the characteristic he most admired in the people he wrote about. His life was, as he titled his first and only novel, "Not Without Laughter."

Perhaps that is why he so loved blues music. He once said, "The mood of the Blues is almost always despondency, but when they are sung people laugh." [1]

Growing Up Black

CHAPTER ONE

Langston Hughes' early life prepared him well to write about humanity, for as a child and young man he lived in many places and met many different kinds of people. His growing-up years were, altogether, not very happy. But they provided him with experiences that many people never have.

James Nathaniel Hughes and Carrie Mercer Langston Hughes would have had a lot going for them—had they been white. James Hughes had studied law, and his wife was a stenographer and at times a newspaperwoman. Their combined salaries would have amounted to a respectable income; they could have taken out a mortgage on a house, had several children, and lived quite comfortably. But the Hughes were black, and because he was black James Hughes could not take the law exam in his home state and start a practice. There were few black lawyers in America in the first years of the twentieth century, and fewer still who could support themselves through the practice of law. White clients would not go to black lawyers, and most black clients could not afford a lawyer. This was certainly the situation in Joplin, Missouri, on February 1, 1902, when James Langston Hughes was born.

From the very first, Langston was a bright, curious child. But his home life was neither very happy nor very secure. His parents did not get along well. There were many arguments about money.

Mr. Hughes was a "penny-pincher"; though they did have to be very careful about money, he seemed to resent even the necessary expenses, except when it came to clothes for himself. A natty dresser, he favored suits with vests and wide-brimmed hats. There were also arguments about moving. Mrs. Hughes thought her husband might be able to find law work in another city. Mr. Hughes was convinced that there was no city in the racially segregated United States where he could find opportunity. He wanted to move his family to Latin America. Finally Mr. Hughes announced he was leaving, and Mrs. Hughes announced she and Langston were staying.

After his father left, Langston and his mother moved around a lot. His mother was always looking for jobs. She preferred night work, for then she could leave Langston by himself, asleep, and during the day she could spend time with him. When his mother had to work during the day, neighbors would care for Langston; but he learned not to grow too close to them, for he knew he and his mother would not stay long.

There were happy times, though. During her free hours Mrs. Hughes would read to Langston and tell him stories, and often she would take him to plays that came to the towns where they lived. His mother loved the theater, and later Langston would learn that she had always secretly wanted to be an actress. She also liked to write, and no matter where they moved she always found a branch of the Interstate Literary Society, an organization which had been founded by her father. She wrote papers and poems to be read at the Society and prepared dramatic readings of famous poems.

Once she chose a poem about a Roman mother with two sons. She was to play the mother, and Langston and another little boy would be her children. She made herself and the two boys Roman-style garments, and together they presented a fine sight. But Langston was not at all happy about being on stage playing a Roman boy. Right in the middle of the reading he began to roll his eyes around and around. The audience twittered. Fearing that she was boring them, Carrie became more intense in her dramatic reading. Langston, his face otherwise expressionless, opened his eyes wider and rolled them faster. Unable to control themselves any longer, some members of the audience burst out laughing, and in seconds the entire auditorium was in an uproar. Later, Langston got a spanking he would never forget. It was not long afterward that Mrs. Hughes decided to move again, this time as much out of embarrassment as out of need for a better job.

When Langston was about six years old, his father wrote from Mexico City to say he wanted his family with him again. Carrie Hughes, tired of her unsettled life, quickly packed up to rejoin her husband. To Langston the journey seemed little different from the others except that it was longer. When he was introduced to the man who was his father, Langston felt a bit awkward. He was just getting used to his father, and to the strange sounds, smells, and voices of Mexico City, when an earthquake hit. As chairs overturned and dishes fell off shelves, Langston ran to his mother for protection. No sooner had the tremors subsided when Mrs. Hughes announced she and Langston were going back to Kansas where people spoke English and where there were no earthquakes!

After returning from Mexico, Mrs. Hughes got a job as a stenographer for a black lawyer in Topeka, Kansas, and rented a room nearby for herself and Langston. Langston was six years old by now, and in September he was due to enter school. The room Mrs. Hughes had rented was in a business district, where few people actually lived. Geographically, though, it fell within a "white" school district, and when Mrs. Hughes tried to enroll Langston she encountered trouble. The district authorities suggested that Langston enroll in the nearest "black" school.

Mrs. Hughes, however, rejected that suggestion. Langston lived closest to the Harrison Street School, and that was the school he would attend. She had to go to the Topeka School Board to get her way, but get it she did.

It was at this time that Langston had his first direct contact with racial prejudice. Some of the children threw rocks at him and chased him home, and one teacher made remarks about his color. It was very hard for the little boy to understand why he was treated so badly. He might easily have become embittered by this experience, but fortunately there were some nice white people at the Harrison Street School as well.

Except for the teacher who made remarks about his color, the teachers in the school were generally kind to him. Some of the white children also took up for him against the others. "So I learned early not to hate *all* white people," Langston would later recall. "And ever since, it has seemed to me that *most* people are generally good, in every race and in every country where I have been." [2]

Mrs. Hughes did not stay in Topeka long. After a little over a year working for the lawyer, she decided to look for a better job in another city. Realizing that Langston could not change schools as often as she changed jobs and cities, she decided that he should live with her mother, at least until she herself settled in one place. So, when he was in second grade, Langston moved once again, this time to his grandmother's house in Lawrence, Kansas.

Langston cried when his mother left. Already he had lived in many different cities and in many different homes, and had come in contact with a great variety of people. Through it all, his mother had been the only constant, stable element. Now even she was gone.

Among the many experiences Langston and his mother had shared were books and reading. Because of her frequent moves, Mrs. Hughes had collected very few possessions. But she always kept a few cherished books with her. Ever since he was a baby she had read to him or encouraged him to read. With his mother gone, Langston naturally turned to one of the things they had shared together—books. He became a frequent visitor to the Lawrence library. Langston would later recall:

> *The silence inside the library, the big chairs, and long tables, and the fact that the library was always there and didn't seem to have a mortgage on it, or any sort of insecurity about it—all of that made me love it. And right then, . . . books began to happen to me, so that after a while, there came a time when I believed in books more than in people—which, of course, was wrong.*[3]

As time went on Langston came to care very much for his grandmother. Mary Sampson Patterson Langston was a proud woman. With her copper-colored skin, long black hair, and aquiline features she looked very Indian. Her grandmother, she said, had been a Cherokee and her grandfather a French trader, so all her people were free. Even during slavery they had free papers and were never in bondage to anyone. She also insisted that she could lay claim to Indian land, although she would always add she would never do so. She never wanted anyone, even the government, to give her something for nothing. She also would not do any work she considered undignified. While she kept her own house spotless, she refused to clean other people's houses, as many black women did. Instead she earned what little income she had from renting out rooms in her house. Sometimes she would rent out the whole house, and she and Langston would stay temporarily with friends. Every penny not spent on food, clothing, or other necessities went toward the monthly mortgage payment on the house. Sometimes the other necessities suffered in favor of the mortgage payment, and there were times when they had very little to eat because of it.

Away in various cities, Langston's mother must have thought often about her son and how lonely he must be without her. One summer she suggested that a friend in Kansas City send her son to stay with Langston for a few weeks. The boy went, but he soon wrote to his mother that he wanted to leave because all he ever ate there was salt pork and dandelions. He also told Langston why he wanted to leave. Langston was only about eight at the time, but he would always remember feeling ashamed of being poor. He never again wanted anyone to stay with him at his grandmother's house.

Mary Sampson Patterson Langston did not mind being poor as much as her little grandson did. For her, owning her own home was worth going hungry sometimes. She represented a group of strong black Americans who refused to accept the second-class citizenship imposed on them by whites. She had been the first black woman to attend Oberlin College in Ohio, and she had married a man equally willing to work toward breaking down the barriers white society had erected around the blacks. Sheridan Leary, her first husband, had been killed fighting with John Brown to free a group of slaves in the famous raid on Harpers Ferry.

Langston's grandmother wished to instill the same kind of pride in her grandson. She often talked to him about what she called his "proud heritage." Most likely, she disliked James Hughes, especially after the breakup of her daughter's marriage. But she made sure Langston knew that James Hughes' grandfather was supposed to have been a relative of the great statesman, Henry Clay. Probably she also grudgingly admired James Hughes for having studied law. In addition, she impressed upon her grandson that her second husband and Langston's grandfather, Charles Langston, had been a politician, and that this man's brother (Langston's great-uncle, John Mercer Langston) had been a congressman from Virginia and later the United States Minister to Haiti. It became quite clear to Langston that he was expected to uphold this heritage.

Mary Langston was a great storyteller, and she told Langston many tales about brave and heroic people—black and white—who had fought against slavery and for black equality. Many years later, Langston would look back on these stories and remember: "Nobody ever cried in my grandmother's stories. They worked, or schemed, or fought. But no crying. When my grandmother died, I didn't cry, either. Something about my grandmother's stories (without her ever having said so) taught me the uselessness of crying about anything." [4]

Langston was twelve when his grandmother died. At her death her house finally went to the mortgage man. In the six years he had lived with his grandmother he had become very attached to her. He missed her very much, and he now felt a great void in his life. With his mother still on the move, Langston was taken in by friends of his grandmother's, whom he called Auntie and Uncle Reed.

There was one thing Langston soon became aware of about Auntie and Uncle Reed. Every Sunday Auntie Reed went to church and Uncle Reed did not. Through them, Langston learned more about the differences among people and not to judge people by such differences. Later he would write, "Both of them were very good and kind—the one who went to church and the one who didn't. And no doubt from them I learned to like Christians and sinners equally well." [5]

But Auntie Reed was relentless in her effort to make Langston "get religion." She had given up trying to convert her husband, but Langston was young and she thought there was still hope for him.

One day she took him to a special children's service that was being held as part of a revival meeting at her church. It was a service for those they called young sinners who had not been brought to Jesus, and Auntie Reed had decided this was the ideal time for Langston to be saved.

Langston had often heard what it was like to be saved. A light came to you, and something happened to you inside. You could see and feel Jesus in your soul, and from then on, wherever you went, God was with you. He had heard this description often from Auntie Reed and from other grown-ups as well. As Langston scrubbed himself as clean as he possibly could and dressed in his best clothes, he had no doubt that on that day at the special service for young sinners he too would join the ranks of the saved.

At the church, the young sinners were seated in the front rows. The rest of the church was crowded with people who had already been saved and had come to sing and pray so that the children might be saved too. It was very hot in the church, but Langston didn't mind. He sat calmly and quietly, waiting for Jesus to come to him.

As the afternoon wore on he watched the other young sinners rise, one by one, to signify that they had seen Jesus. Each time, the congregation exploded with joy, welcoming the new convert with open arms and rejoicing. Now, only one other boy and Langston remained on the front benches. They looked at each other. Then the other boy stood up. That left Langston by himself, and he felt very small and very alone. All around him people prayed for his salvation. Auntie Reed was among them, crying, because he was the only one not yet saved.

Langston had not seen Jesus. He had seen no light, and nothing had happened to him inside. But he was ashamed of himself for holding everyone up for so long. At last, like the others before him, Langston stood. Instantly the church was filled with cries of joy. Only Langston felt no joy.

That night, for almost the last time in his life, Langston cried. He cried in anger. He was angry with Jesus for not coming to help him. But he was angrier with himself for pretending to have had an experience he really had not. He had been forced to disappoint either himself or other people, and he did not think he had made the right choice.

It was during another event at his aunt's church that he found that disappointing other people and not himself was not exactly the right choice either. He had been chosen to recite a poem at a special Children's Day program at the church and did not want to do it. Even though he knew the poem by heart, and even though his mother had come all the way from Kansas City to hear him, after reciting a few lines he stopped and just stood there. Frantically, in loud stage whispers, his aunt tried to prompt him. But he pretended not to hear. Finally, after a long, embarrassed silence, he returned to his seat. His aunt and his mother were angry, and deep inside Langston was probably sorry for embarrassing them. But he had a stubborn streak in him that caused him to stick to a decision no matter what. While it got him into trouble at times it would also serve him well.

The school Langston attended in Lawrence was for blacks, and since both his grandmother and the Reeds lived in a black neighborhood, he did not have much contact with whites or with racial prejudice. Certainly he went into the business and shopping districts at times, and he loved to go to the movies, but he did not experience any obvious prejudice until he was about thirteen. He was in the seventh grade and had managed to get a job in the old hotel in his neighborhood cleaning the toilets, keeping the mirrors shined, and emptying the spittoons. He worked after school, and with the fifty cents a week he earned he went to the movies on Saturdays. One Saturday he made his way to the theater as usual, but as he approached the entrance, something brought him up short. There, posted on the front of the building, was a large sign: NO COLORED ADMITTED. Langston stood there for a while, bewildered and angry, gazing at the sign. He wondered why the management had suddenly decided to close the theater to blacks. He'd never misbehaved there and he didn't remember seeing any other blacks acting rowdy. It was unfair—now how was he going to get to see any movies?

Langston walked slowly back to the Reed's house and went straight to his room. He wished his grandmother were still alive. She would have been able to make him feel better. She would have reminded him of the brave black people she had known who would not have allowed such an incident to make them feel badly. She would have warned him not to be bitter, but to determine to do something about it when he grew older. But his grandmother was dead, and Langston had to deal with his hurt alone.

CHAPTER TWO

Two years after his grandmother died, when Langston was nearly fourteen, his mother sent for him to join her in Lincoln, Illinois. She had remarried and had a new baby, and now felt she could provide a stable home for her son. Langston was pleased to be with his mother again, and he enjoyed his baby half brother, Kit. He also liked his stepfather, Homer Clark, who was working as a cook when Langston joined the family. After settling into an integrated school where he got along well, Langston began to let himself hope that the arrangement would be permanent.

Before long, however, Homer Clark announced he was tired of being a cook and making so little money. The United States had recently entered World War I, and northern factories were booming in the production of war materials. Since there were plenty of jobs in these factories, Homer decided to go to Cleveland, Ohio, to find work. Once he had a job and got settled, he would send for his family. He was in Cleveland when Langston graduated from grammar school.

In honor of this graduation Langston wrote his first poem, although it was certainly not his idea to do so. Somehow it had become a tradition in the school that each graduating class should have a Class Poet, and Langston was chosen. He had never before written a poem, but then, neither had anyone else in the class. Langston later explained why he was chosen: "In America most white people think, of course, that *all* Negroes can sing and dance, and have a sense of rhythm. So my classmates, knowing that a poem had to have rhythm, elected me unanimously—thinking, no doubt, that I had some, being a Negro." [6]

Langston thought about the kind of poem he should write. Naturally, since it was to be read at graduation, it should be about the school, the teachers, and the class. The most popular teacher, and Langston's favorite, was Miss Ethel Welsh, and he started by writing a nice verse about her. But having written a verse about one teacher, he realized he had to be fair and write a verse about each one. With those completed he had eight verses. If the teachers had eight verses, the class should have eight too, he decided. It was the longest poem Langston would ever write!

The poem was a great success, and of course it could not have been otherwise, since it praised the school, the teachers, and the graduating class as the best ever. The applause pleased Langston. He realized how much he had enjoyed writing the poem, even though he knew it wasn't a very good one. He didn't have a wide basis of comparison; the only poems he had liked as a child were *Hiawatha* and those of black poet Paul Laurence Dunbar. But he did know there was a lot more to poetry than merely a series of rhyming verses.

Not long after Langston's graduation, Homer Clark sent for his family to join him in Cleveland, where he had gotten a job working in a steel mill. He had tried to find comfortable quarters for them, but they were just not to be had—not at a steelworker's wage. Cleveland, like many other northern industrial towns during World War I, was filled to overflowing with people looking for work. Thousands of Southern blacks had migrated to these cities, and the black residential areas were just not large enough to accommodate them. Houses and apartments were divided and subdivided, and exorbitant rents were charged for cubbyholes. Langston and his family were forced to live first in an attic and then in a basement.

These may not have been the best conditions to foster a budding poet, but somehow Langston managed to find a corner now and then where he could shut out the people and noise around him and try to put his feelings down on paper. Though he wasn't very pleased with his attempts, he did not give up.

In the fall, Langston entered Cleveland's Central High School. Its students were predominantly first-generation Americans, sons and daughters of immigrants from Poland and elsewhere in Eastern Europe, who felt very little antiblack prejudice. Perhaps they respected the black people's long tradition in America. In fact, these students were much more concerned with religious differences, for example, Jews versus gentiles, than with the differences between races. For his part, Langston had both Jewish and non-Jewish white friends. Being neither himself, he was elected to a number of student offices.

Among the several teachers at Central High who influenced Langston, his favorite was his English teacher, Miss Weimer. Noting his interest in poetry she introduced him to the works of Carl Sandburg, Vachel Lindsay, Amy Lowell, and many others. She also encouraged him to submit his poems to the school magazine, the *Belfry Owl.*

Langston was busy writing a lot of poetry by now, and his best poems were those about things he knew, things he saw, or things that happened to him or to those around him. Homer Clark was very unhappy in his job at the steel mill, for it was dirty, back-breaking work which left him exhausted and irritable by the end of the day. Langston's response to this was a poem he wrote when he was about fourteen, called "The Mills":

The mills
That grind and grind,
That grind out steel
And grind away the lives
Of men—
In the sunset their stacks
Are great black silhouettes
Against the sky.
In the dawn
They belch red fire.
The mills—
Grinding new steel,
Old men.

He also wrote short black dialect poems after the style of black poet Paul Laurence Dunbar, trying to capture in verse the rhythm of the dialect:

Just because I loves you—
That's de reason why
My soul is full of color
Like de wings of a butterfly.

Just because I loves you
That's de reason why
My heart's a fluttering aspen leaf
When you pass by.

Toward the end of Langston's sophomore year at Central, his mother and stepfather separated, and his mother took Kit, his young half brother, to Chicago. Langston did not want to leave Central, so he got a summer job to earn enough money to stay in Cleveland by himself.

Langston was very proud of being on his own when only a junior in high school, but he certainly didn't find it as glamorous as he had expected. Certainly, he didn't have to answer to anyone, but then there was no one to cook for him either. He couldn't afford to eat in restaurants, so he had to cook in the kitchen of the house where he roomed. And, since the only things he knew how to cook were hot dogs and rice, he ate hot dogs and rice every single night.

Moreover he was quite lonely. When he was at school with the others during the day he did not feel it so much. But sometimes after school, when he returned home to his small room, the hours seemed to stretch endlessly before him. Because books had consoled him in his loneliness many times before in his life, he began to read a great deal. He read nonfiction and fiction by both American and foreign writers. He especially enjoyed short stories, and he marveled at the ability of someone like the French writer Guy de Maupassant to write stories that were so true to life that people in other countries read them. Secretly, Langston wanted very much to write stories like that, stories about black people that would have the same universal quality and would be read by people all over the world. But he did not dare try to write such stories

—he just did not feel he could. He did write a story about a Polish girl entitled "Mary Winosky" when he was a junior, but he just did not feel comfortable writing stories.

Poems were another matter. They came to him easily now, and whenever one came to him he would scribble it down on a scrap of paper, a napkin, whatever was within reach. Later, he would copy it over in a notebook. Poems he thought were especially good he sent to national magazines, but they always came back with rejection slips.

Toward the end of his junior year at Central, Langston received an astonishing message. His father wanted him to spend the summer with him in Mexico. Langston had not seen James Hughes for over ten years, and the thought of traveling to Mexico was exciting. Despite his mother's disapproval, as soon as the school term was over Langston boarded a train bound for Mexico City.

Langston was a little taken aback when his father met him at the train. Hardly the strong, bronze cowboy he had pictured, his father was a small, nattily dressed man who spoke in clipped sentences and always seemed in a hurry. In fact, "Hurry up!" was his favorite expression. In Langston's opinion, he was also a snob. James Hughes wasted no time in telling his son what he thought of poor people. He criticized blacks in the United States, saying they were lazy and moved around too much and did not try to better themselves. He disliked poor Mexicans too. In fact, he had no use for anyone who wasn't successful, as he was.

James Hughes had been practicing law in Mexico. He had invested in property and lent money, charging interest, to other people. And he wanted Langston to be a successful businessman like himself. When Langston told his father that he wrote poetry and wanted to write stories, his father frowned, saying that writing was no career. Before long Langston realized that his stay in Mexico was not going to be very pleasant.

His father had a house outside Mexico City in Toluca, a high valley beneath white volcanoes. The house and adjacent stables were attended by a housekeeper and a stable boy, who both disliked James Hughes fully as much as Langston did. In fact, the only people who did like his father were three maiden ladies who lived together in Mexico City and who had helped James when he had arrived in Mexico many years before.

Nearly every day Mr. Hughes went away to inspect his properties and conduct other business. But Langston's time was not his own when his father was away. Every day before he left Mr. Hughes would assign Langston a number of difficult bookkeeping problems to solve. His father would not accept the excuse that Langston was not good in math, and so every day Langston would labor for hours on figures that made no sense to him and problems he had no desire to solve. And all the while, he could hear his father's voice saying, "Hurry up!"

Langston did not rebel. In many ways he was afraid of his father, for he could not understand him. He searched for some hint of warmth or compassion in his father, and, finding none, felt very alone. He kept hoping for a letter from his mother, but she did not write. By the middle of July Langston was deep in despair. He even considered suicide: "One day, when there was no one in the house but me," he would later recall, "I put the pistol to my head and held it there, loaded, a long time, and wondered if I would be any happier if I were to pull the trigger. But then, I began to think, if I do, I might miss something. I haven't been to the ranch yet, nor to the top of the volcano, nor to the bullfights in Mexico City, nor graduated from high school, nor got married. So I put the pistol down and went back to my bookkeeping." [7]

Ever since he had arrived, Langston had been asking his father to take him to his ranch a few miles away and to Mexico City, but his father had refused again and again, saying that he wanted Langston to learn bookkeeping. Shortly after the pistol incident James Hughes noticed how depressed his son was and offered to take him to Mexico City for a week. Langston got so excited that, even though they were not to leave for another ten days, he began to pack. But his son's excitement did not soften Mr. Hughes' attitude any further. If anything, it became harsher. It seemed to Langston that his father said, "Hurry up!" twice as often in those ten days than he had before, and that the bookkeeping problems he assigned were even more difficult. Fearful that his father might change his mind if he did anything to displease him, Langston worked harder than ever. By the morning of the trip he was a nervous wreck.

His father woke him before dawn. "Hurry up and get dressed," he said. Minutes later came the order, "Hurry up and eat." But Langston could not eat. His stomach began to churn with the rage he felt against his father turned inward. Langston did go to Mexico City, but not to the bullfights; he went to an American hospital there for several weeks, suffering from a stomach infection. And when he learned that his father was spending twenty dollars a day to keep him in the hospital, Langston made no attempt at all to get better. It served his penny-pinching father right, he decided.

In the fall, with great relief, Langston returned to Cleveland. His father now sent him an allowance, which enabled him to rent a room and to eat something other than hot dogs and rice. But while he had fewer financial worries this year than the last, there were other things to worry him. World War I ended in November, and conditions changed for the blacks who lived in the previously quite liberal city of Cleveland. It was as if prejudice had been put aside during the crisis of wartime, but with the war over people had nothing better to do than to revive old prejudices. The factories slowed down production, and many black workers were laid off; returning white soldiers were given first preference in being hired for new jobs. Restaurants and theaters began refusing to admit blacks, and Langston was painfully reminded of his experience at the theater in Lawrence five years before.

Fortunately for Langston, young people did not respond to the winds of prejudice as quickly as the adults had. To his classmates, Langston was the same person who had started high school with them, and it was a happy year for him in school. As a senior, he was editor of the school yearbook, and he began to go with a girl recently up from the South. He wrote a poem about her, and in it he incorporated the gospel and jazz rhythms that would later come to characterize his poetry:

When Susanna Jones wears red
Her face is like an ancient cameo
Turned brown by the ages.

Come with a blast of trumpets,
Jesus!

When Susanna Jones wears red
A queen from some time-dead Egyptian night
Walks once again.

Blow trumpets, Jesus!

And the beauty of Susanna Jones in red
Burns in my heart a love-fire sharp like pain.

Sweet silver trumpets,
Jesus!

By now Langston had a whole notebook full of poems and another of verses and jingles. At graduation he was named Class Poet—this time with good reason.

In Search of a Life-Style

CHAPTER THREE

At the invitation of his father, Langston returned to Mexico after graduation. Though reluctant to do so, he really had no better place to go. He had not done much thinking about his future, and graduating had been a rather unsettling experience. Before, he had always had another school year to look forward to. Many of his graduating classmates still did, for they were going to college. Langston wanted to go to college too, but he just did not have the money for it. The only one with money for his college education was his father, and Langston was practical enough to realize it would be foolish to alienate his father, no matter how much he disliked him. The only drawback was that in returning to Mexico Langston again angered his mother. Failing to understand that he needed her support, she once again refused to approve of the trip.

The train ride to Mexico was long and unhappy for Langston. He was angry and hurt by his mother's attitude, and he dreaded seeing his father again. He felt sick to his stomach just thinking about his father's constant criticism of their own people. As he looked out the train window at the brown, rushing waters of the Mississippi, he thought about the generations of black people who had worked along its banks—black people who remained poor despite their hard work. It occurred to him that his people were like the Mississippi—flowing along, sometimes turbulent, sometimes calm, getting muddy along the way, but always enduring. And he thought about other rivers that black people had known, in other places and in other times, and a poem came to him. It would prove to be one of his most famous:

THE NEGRO SPEAKS OF RIVERS

I've known rivers:
I've known rivers ancient as the world and older than
the flow of human blood in human veins.

My soul has grown deep like the rivers.

I bathed in the Euphrates when dawns were young.
I built my hut near the Congo and it lulled me to sleep.
I looked upon the Nile and raised the pyramids above it.
I heard the singing of the Mississippi when Abe
Lincoln went down to New Orleans, and I've seen
its muddy bosom turn all golden in the sunset.

I've known rivers:
Ancient, dusky rivers.

My soul has grown deep like the rivers.

Langston wanted to attend Columbia University, not because he knew much about the university itself, but because it was in New York City, and also in New York City was Harlem. The very name "Harlem" had a magical sound to Langston, as it did to many young blacks across America. Harlem was where the action was, where there were more black people concentrated in one area than anywhere else in America, and where the sophisticated blacks were. Of course he did not intend to tell his father this. He planned to broach the subject of Columbia gradually and at an opportune time.

Langston's plans did not work out, however, for shortly after his arrival his father announced that Langston would attend college in Switzerland and then go to a German engineering school to become a mining engineer. A mining engineer! Langston protested, saying he wanted to be a writer, but Mr. Hughes declared that he would not spend one penny for Langston to go to any college in the United States and that Langston could just stay in Mexico until he acquired some sense.

Meanwhile, Langston continued to write, and some of his best-known poems came out of this period. "For my best poems were all written when I felt the worst," Langston would later explain. "When I was happy, I didn't write anything." [8] He also wrote other things besides poems—an article about Toluca, an article about the Virgin of Guadalupe, and a children's play, for instance. These he sent to *Brownie's Book*, a magazine for black children, which, to his delight accepted the works. What's more, the *Crisis*, the parent magazine of *Brownie's Book*, published his poem "The Negro Speaks of Rivers." Though he was not paid by these magazines, his work was at least now appearing in publications with national circulation. Moreover, the acceptance of his work for publication probably helped convince James Hughes to give in to his son's desire to go to Columbia.

That spring, however, a strange and violent event occurred at the house in Toluca, which almost prevented Langston from going to Columbia—or anywhere else, for that matter. Frau Schultz, Mr. Hughes' German housekeeper, was friendly with the housekeeper of the town's brewery-master. The brewery-master's housekeeper had a pretty young daughter named Gerta, whom the brewery-master was in love with. Often Gerta would visit Frau Schultz at the Hughes' home, and the brewery-master, a very jealous man, believed Gerta was really visiting Langston.

This was not at all true. Certainly Langston was acquainted with Gerta, but when she came to visit she stayed with the older women. Langston was often out or elsewhere in the house, writing. He did not even speak German, and she spoke neither English nor Spanish. Had he known that the brewery-master was jealous of him, he probably would have stayed away from Gerta altogether.

One day Gerta and her mother visited Frau Schultz while Langston was away in town. But the brewery-master did not know this. Unable to contain his jealousy any longer, he followed them to the Hughes' home. The three women, who sat talking in the Hughes' parlor, suspected nothing. The brewery-master burst into the room, gun blazing wildly.

When Langston returned home a half hour later, he could

hardly believe what had happened. All three women had been shot, and Gerta was in critical condition. It was a miracle that she survived at all. It was a miracle, too, Langston thought, that he had not been there when it happened. He shuddered to think that if he had returned a little earlier he might not have lived to tell the story.

One day in early September, 1921, James Hughes took his son to Mexico City, where Langston boarded a train for Vera Cruz; from there he would take a boat to New York. As the train pulled away from the station, Langston watched the receding figure of his father standing on the platform, and as the man grew smaller, so did Langston's concern with him. Certainly he was grateful to his father for sending him to college. But that did not make up for the way James Hughes had treated him.

For the first time in his life Langston felt free—really free. He did not have to worry about money or answer to anyone, and he was on his way to Harlem! When people are very happy, they forever after associate their surroundings of that time with pleasure. The wide expanse of blue-green sea, the smell of the salt-sea air, the sounds of seabirds, and the splash of the waves against the moving boat mingled with Langston's feelings of joy. It was his first experience with the sea, and it would make a lasting impression on him.

Equally memorable to Langston were his first glimpse of the New York skyline, looming up from the horizon to what seemed unbelievable heights, and his first sight of Harlem, to which he made his way the morning after the boat docked. He would later say:

> *I can never put on paper the thrill of that underground ride to Harlem. I had never been in a subway before and it fascinated me—the noise, the speed, the green lights ahead. At every station I kept watching for the sign:* 135TH STREET. *When I saw it, I held my breath. I came out onto the platform with two heavy bags and looked around. It was still early morning and people were going to work. Hundreds of colored people! I wanted to shake hands with them, speak to them. I hadn't seen*

Langston Hughes as a young man, 1923

any colored people for so long—that is, any Negro colored people.[9]

Langston reacted to Harlem the way many young blacks before and after him did, especially those not used to big cities. Harlem was the largest black community in the United States, and it pulsated with energy. Its streets teemed with people, night and day. Its stores displayed everything one could possibly want, and it was hard to imagine there could be enough people to buy all those items. Music was everywhere on the main streets—music and laughter and loud voices. The community was bustling with postwar prosperity; pride showed on the faces of the people. This was their community.

And it was a community in every sense of the word. Organizations, brotherhoods, and self-help societies abounded. Hardly a weekend went by when there wasn't a parade of some sort. There was a sense of possibility, of opportunity, which acted as a powerful magnet to young, talented black people all over the country. Although Langston had no way of knowing it at the time, what would become the largest pool of black creative talent in history was just then beginning to converge upon Harlem.

Langston would have liked nothing better than to stay in Harlem and forget about going to Columbia. He only checked into the dormitory at the beginning of the term because his father had already paid the tuition, room, and board. Once there, he wished he had followed his initial instincts, for he was not at all welcome in the dormitory. They had thought he was Mexican! Ironically, a nonwhite foreigner was more welcome there than a native-born American black. The following term Langston moved into the YMCA in Harlem.

Columbia was a very large university, and from the start Langston was unhappy there. Since he was not outgoing it was hard for him to make friends with the other students. And classes were so large that he could not get to know his instructors personally. Also he was very conscious of being one of the only black students on campus. Years later he would write a poem expressing his unhappiness there, calling it "Theme for English B":

The instructor said,

Go home and write
a page tonight.
And let that page come out of you—
Then, it will be true.

I wonder if it's that simple?
I am twenty-two, colored, born in Winston-Salem.
I went to school there, then Durham, then here
to this college on the hill above Harlem.
I am the only colored student in my class.
The steps from the hill lead down into Harlem,
through a park, then across St. Nicholas,
Eighth Avenue, Seventh, and I come to the Y,
the Harlem Branch Y, where I take the elevator
up to my room, sit down, and write this page:

It's not easy to know what is true for you or me
at twenty-two, my age. But I guess I'm what
I feel and see and hear, Harlem, I hear you:
hear you, hear me—we two—you, me, talk on this page.
(I heard New York, too.) Me—who?

Well, I like to eat, sleep, drink, and be in love.
I like to work, read, learn, and understand life.
I like a pipe for a Christmas present,
or records—Bessie, bop, or Bach.
I guess being colored doesn't make me *not* like
the same things other folks like who are other races.
So will my page be colored that I write?

Being me, it will not be white.
But it will be
a part of you, instructor.
You are white—
yet a part of me, as I am a part of you.
That's American.
Sometimes perhaps you don't want to be a part of me.
Nor do I often want to be a part of you.
But we are, that's true!
As I learn from you,
I guess you learn from me—
although you're older—and white—
and somewhat more free.

This is my page for English B.

THE CRISIS

A RECORD OF THE DARKER RACES

Volume One NOVEMBER, 1910 Number One

Edited by W. E. BURGHARDT DU BOIS, with the co-operation of Oswald Garrison Villard, J. Max Barber, Charles Edward Russell, Kelly Miller, W. S. Braithwaite and M. D. Maclean.

CONTENTS

PUBLISHED MONTHLY BY THE

National Association for the Advancement of Colored People

AT TWENTY VESEY STREET NEW YORK CITY

ONE DOLLAR A YEAR TEN CENTS A COPY

The Crisis, a magazine for blacks founded by W. E. B. Du Bois

At first Langston did try to do the work that was required of him, but as time went on he studied less and less. He spent a lot of time writing poetry and sending what he considered his best poems to the *Crisis*. This magazine had been started by the eminent black scholar and writer W. E. B. Du Bois for the purpose of serving as a forum for black artistic and political thought. *Brownie's Book*, an offspring of the *Crisis*, had first published Langston's writings; now the *Crisis* was also publishing them. During that year at Columbia he had even been invited to luncheon once by an editor at the *Crisis* and had met several of the magazine's staff. While he was flattered by the invitation and liked the people he met, Langston was very uncomfortable, for he felt unsophisticated and not very bright around such learned people.

Then his mother and Kit came to New York, and Langston had to support them on his allowance until he could find a job for his mother and a place to live for all of them. By the time this was accomplished he was way behind in his studies and did not even care. He was reading, but not the books assigned, and spending his allowance on shows. Though he finished the year with passing grades, he was just not interested in continuing school. He wrote his father that he was going to quit school and find a job. His father never answered the letter—and never again sent any money either.

After the school year ended, Langston worked on a truck farm on Staten Island and at a florist in Manhattan.

"But all those months in New York I'd kept remembering the smell of the sea on my first night in Vera Cruz," Langston would later write. "And it seemed to me now that if I had to work for low wages at dull jobs, I might just as well see the world, so I began to look for work on a ship." [10]

In those days just about the only place on a ship where a black person could get work was in the galley, but Langston did not mind. When the opportunity came to sign on with a ship as mess boy, he could not scribble his signature fast enough. Shortly, though, he wished he had had sense enough to ask first where the ship was going. To his dismay he found that his ship would be going no more than a few miles away—and that certainly didn't cover much of the world!

His ship was one of the "mother ships" belonging to the "mothball" fleet, a group of poorly built World War I ships that had been towed up the Hudson and put at anchor. Though the ships were not to be used in the near future, it was necessary to keep their machinery oiled and to prevent them from drifting away or being vandalized. About four of the eighty or so ships were manned by skeleton crews. Langston's job was to help feed his crew and take care of their laundry and quarters.

It was a long, lonely winter that Langston spent on the Hudson. Sometimes no sound could be heard but the howling winds and the creaking of chains as the ships strained against their anchors in the stormy waters. With such a small crew, Langston's duties were minimal, and he had lots of time to himself. He wrote many poems that winter, and it was then that he wrote one of his most famous.

For nearly as long as he could remember, Langston had been fascinated by black music, especially blues. It seemed to express for him the sadness and pain and capacity to endure that characterized black people of America. During that lonely winter on the Hudson, Langston tried to write about the music and to capture the rhythm of it in a poem. He probably worked harder on this poem than on any other; he wrote and rewrote and rewrote again. He called his poem "The Weary Blues," and it began:

Droning a drowsy syncopated tune,
Rocking back and forth to a mellow croon,
    I heard a Negro play.
Down on Lenox Avenue the other night
By the pale dull pallor of an old gas light
    He did a lazy sway. . . .
    He did a lazy sway. . . .
To the tune o' those Weary Blues.
With his ebony hands on each ivory key
He made that poor piano moan with melody.
    O Blues!
Swaying to and fro on his rickety stool
He played that sad raggy tune like a musical fool.
    Sweet Blues!
Coming from a black man's soul.
    O Blues!

The poem also included the first blues verse he had ever heard. He had been only a child, in Lawrence, Kansas, but the verse had so impressed him that he had remembered it ever since:

"I got the Weary Blues
And I can't be satisfied.
Got the Weary Blues
And can't be satisfied—
I ain't happy no mo'
And I wish that I had died."

For Langston that verse summed up the conditions of black life.

Except for his writing "The Weary Blues," only two things worthy of note happened to Langston that long, lonely winter. The first was the night spent on a "haunted" ship.

Among the empty ships that Langston's "mother ship" watched over was one on which there had been a mutiny during the war and the captain of the ship had been killed. Bullet holes could still be seen in the steel plates of the bridge. The sailors on the mother ship insisted that ghosts still walked there at night. Langston declared that he did not believe in ghosts, but the sailors insisted that if he ever spent a night on the ship he would turn white with fear. Langston realized the crew's notions had come from seeing too many movies in which blacks were portrayed as inordinately afraid of the supernatural and had, through cinematic techniques, indeed "turned white with fear." So he decided to prove the stereotype wrong and spent one entire night on the unlit, unheated ship, emerging, of course, unharmed. He had disproved the stereotype but, after such an uncomfortable night, he must have wondered if it had been worth it.

The second event of note was that during the winter Langston received a letter from Alain Locke, a well-known black writer, poet, and scholar, asking to visit Langston. Locke had seen and been impressed by a poem of Langston's that had appeared in the *Crisis*. Surprising as it may seem, Langston said no. Remembering the luncheon with the *Crisis* staff, he was afraid he would feel inferior in the company of such a great man. Even though Locke could have helped him in his writing career, Langston could not bring himself to meet the man.

Dr. Alain Locke

When spring came Langston quit his job with the mothball fleet, this time determined to sign on with a ship that was *going* somewhere. With fine recommendations from his boss, the ship's steward, he got a job on a cargo ship sailing for Africa.

The night the ship sailed Langston looked over the belongings he had brought on board with him. Among other things was a box of books he had left in storage in Harlem the previous fall. He had intended to keep them. "But," he later wrote, "when I opened them up and looked at them that night off Sandy Hook, they seemed too much like everything I had known in the past, like the attics and basements in Cleveland, like the lonely nights in Toluca, like the dormitory at Columbia, like the furnished room in Harlem, like too much reading all the time when I was a kid, like life isn't, as described in romantic prose; . . . the memory of my father, the poverty and uncertainties of my mother's life, the stupidities of color prejudice, black in a white world, the fear of not finding a job, the bewilderment of no one to talk to about things that trouble you, the feeling of always being controlled by others—by parents, by employers, by some outer necessity not your own. All those things I wanted to throw away. . . . I was twenty-one. So I threw the books in the sea." [11]

CHAPTER FOUR

Langston was very excited about going to Africa, the homeland of his ancestors. He would now really get to see the rivers he had imagined and written about in "The Negro Speaks of Rivers." He thought he was prepared for the sights of Africa, but as he approached the coastline he was astonished by its incredible beauty, its gleaming shores, its sun-dappled trees, and its feeling of nature gone wild. He envied the people of Africa their rich land, and he envied them more their long, unbroken heritage.

Once the ship had docked, however, Langston was able to see the ugliness that, ever since the coming of Europeans, was Africa too. He saw African riches being shipped out to Europe and America. He saw white Europeans driving African work gangs with whips. He saw signs warning EUROPEANS ONLY. He saw all around him disease, poverty, and despair.

Langston identified with the Africans, believing their problems to be similar to those of blacks in the United States. But when he tried to tell them that he was really one of them, they only laughed. They looked at his copper-colored skin and wavy hair—and insisted he was white! Most of them had not seen many American blacks, and as there was little white blood in them, they were not aware of the wide range of skin shades among American blacks.

When Langston's ship sailed for America, it carried a rich cargo —black palm oil, cocoa beans, and mahogany. And Langston, on the ship, carried away something rich too—a sense of pride that he had not felt before. He deplored the exploitation he had seen but felt a kind of completeness as a black American who had returned to his homeland, if only as a visitor.

Langston carried back something else as well—a big red monkey for which he had paid three shillings, an old shirt, and a pair of shoes. He named him Jocko and planned to present him to his half brother, Kit. Almost all the sailors had bought either a parrot or a monkey. In fact, there were some twenty monkeys on board ship on the return voyage to America. At the captain's order, a large cage was built for them on deck. They were fed scraps left over from the sailors' meals. While off-duty each crew member who owned one could take his monkey out of the cage for exercise. Jocko, who at first hated Langston and bit him at every opportunity, grew to love his owner. Before long Jocko would go into a temper whenever Langston tried to put him down!

Everything went well until the ship ran into a storm. Waves washed over the deck, and a huge one hit the monkey cage and broke it open. Monkeys of all shapes and sizes screamed and dashed about for cover. Many invaded the passengers' quarters, sending the frightened people scurrying for safety. Some monkeys managed to get into the captain's room and took not only his pencils but also a portion of the ship's records aloft to the mastheads. It took two days to round up all the monkeys, and Langston's Jocko was one of the last to be captured.

Langston's family was now living in McKeesport, Pennsylvania, near Pittsburgh, and Langston visited them there for a week. His stay was quite pleasant except for one thing—his mother's reaction to Jocko. She hated the monkey from the moment she saw him, and the first night of Langston's stay she locked them both in a bedroom.

Jocko's antics did not help the situation—he scampered over the furniture and bit anyone who tried to pick him up except Langston. After a while, Jocko and Kit got to know each other, and Langston hoped his mother would take to the monkey. But even if she had wanted to it would have been pretty hard, for Jocko seemed bent on making life miserable for her. He would leap at her apron strings until he had untied them. He would take buttons and thimbles from her sewing box and put them in his mouth. But his favorite trick was to fill his mouth with phonograph needles, then spit them out all over the place. When Langston returned to New York and left the monkey there, he worried what might happen between Jocko and his mother. He was later saddened to learn that soon after he left, his mother sold his little monkey friend.

Back in New York, Langston got a job on a ship bound for Istanbul and Odessa. But he never sailed on that ship. As he and the other mess attendants were loading supplies on board, the chief steward fell and broke his arm. The new chief steward did not like blacks, so Langston and the other black mess attendants were replaced by whites. A month later the ship hit a floating mine left over from World War I, and half the crew drowned. After that, it seemed to Langston that the results of prejudice were not always in his disfavor!

After an unhappy stint on an ugly ship that sailed to and from the West Indies, Langston signed on to a ship that ran between New York and Rotterdam. But while his first round trip was pleasant, the second trip to Rotterdam seemed jinxed. The ship was buffeted about by terrible storms, the chief engineer died of double pneumonia, and the radio operator had a mental breakdown. It was just too much. When the ship reached Rotterdam, Langston collected the twenty-five dollars' pay and quit. He then headed for Paris.

It was probably because of Guy de Maupassant that Langston had first longed to see Paris. Later he heard that it was a place where discrimination against blacks was practically nonexistent, and that many black Americans lived there. So, finding himself in Rotterdam, jobless, and with twenty-five dollars to spend, it was natural that he should buy a ticket on the night train for Paris.

Langston's first experience of Paris was not quite what he had expected, and he wished he would not always get his hopes up about things. While the Parisians did not appear racist, they were condescending when they heard his labored, high-school French. Americans find foreign accents attractive; Parisians do not. The people spoke so rapidly that Langston had great difficulty understanding them. He learned that most of the American blacks in the city lived in the section of Montmartre. But he felt no more welcome there than he did in downtown Paris. He would have considerable trouble finding a job, other Americans told him, if he wasn't either a musician or a tap dancer.

It took Langston an entire month to find a job, and he nearly starved before he got it. He was hired as doorman for a little nightclub in Montmartre at a salary of five francs (less than a quarter) per night and dinner. Langston was so hungry he requested the dinner immediately. One full meal and a bottle of wine later, he took up his position at the door of the nightclub and promptly fell asleep.

While he wasn't fired for that incident, Langston did not stay with the job very long. He soon learned that he was expected to be a bouncer as well, to stop fights and throw out belligerent customers. This was not at all to Langston's liking, for he had never been aggressive, and when another job came along he grabbed it.

The job was as second-cook at a well-known nightclub. Though he still didn't know how to cook anything but hot dogs and rice, he had learned through hard experience that if you had a chance for a job you said you could do it and worried about actually doing it later. Langston was relieved to learn that the job was really dishwashing, and that he could do.

His salary was not high, but it was adequate for his needs, and breakfast was included. He liked the other employees, and he stayed on the job for some months. Feeling very artistic in a rented room in a Paris garret, Langston would sit by his window, which looked out over the red tile rooftops of the city, and write poetry. Then, with the coming of spring, he lived yet another romantic Paris illusion—he fell in love.

Mary was an English-African girl who lived in the Latin Quarter. She was wealthy, educated, pretty, and very nice, and Langston was certain he had found the girl he would marry. Mary's father, however, had other ideas. He wanted his daughter to marry an

African official in the colonial service of the English government. When he discovered that his daughter was in love with a poor American black, he had her removed to London. Langston never saw her again. One day, he wrote a poem about her called "The Breath of a Rose":

Love is like dew
On lilacs at dawn:
Comes the swift sun
And the dew is gone.

Love is like star-light
In the sky at morn:
Star-light that dies
When day is born.

Love is like perfume
In the heart of a rose:
The flower withers,
The perfume goes—

Love is no more
Than the breath of a rose,
No more
Than the breath of a rose.

Langston would have other girl friends, but he would never marry. Later in his life he would come to understand that he was homosexual.

After Mary left, Langston slept a great deal, for then he did not have to think of her so often. Anyway he was trying to save money, and while he was sleeping he didn't feel the need to eat. One day he was awakened by a knock at his door. Eyes half open, clothes disheveled, he opened the door to none other than Dr. Alain Locke, the man he had refused to meet back in New York. Locke was not intimidating at all, but very warm and down-to-earth. He was in Europe on vacation and had gotten Langston's address from the people at the *Crisis*. He wanted to see some of Langston's poems for possible use in a special black issue of *Survey Graphic*, a major U.S. magazine of the day. After Locke left, Langston thought how foolish had been his fear of meeting Locke. He realized that while all great people were not as charming as Locke, one should not necessarily feel uncomfortable around them.

Claude McKay

In July two of the waiters at the nightclub where Langston worked invited him home to Italy with them for a vacation. Langston was still very depressed over the loss of Mary, and he decided it might be good for him to get away from Paris.

Langston enjoyed the few weeks spent with his friends and their families, although in one town he found himself something of an attraction as the first black person the people there had ever seen. He and Locke were corresponding now, and after Langston thanked his hosts and struck out on his own, he spent some time in Venice with Locke. While in Venice Locke suggested that Langston go to visit a young black American writer named Claude McKay who was living on the Riviera, and, after notifying McKay that he was coming, Langston boarded a train in Venice bound for the Riviera.

But he never reached the Riviera. Shortly after the train left Venice he fell asleep, and when he awoke he discovered he had been robbed—his money, his passport, everything. Unwilling to show up penniless at McKay's door, he decided to return to America instead.

Getting a job on a ship out of Genoa was nearly impossible, for most American ships would not hire blacks. The few lire the thieves had left him were spent quickly, and Langston went hungry many days in Genoa. He seriously considered stealing food but never actually did. At last he got an idea. He would write an article about his trip to Africa to send to the *Crisis,* with a note explaining his plight and asking them to please pay him twenty dollars. It would be the first time he would ask the *Crisis* to pay him for his work. When the article was finished, he sent it off and waited.

Several days went by, but nothing came, and when a ship that did hire blacks turned up, he signed on with it. His pay would be merely his passage back to America. Arriving in New York, Langston had only a quarter in his pocket.

But soon after he had twenty dollars. The people at the *Crisis* had cabled him the twenty dollars, but it had come back to them, unclaimed. Feeling that he deserved the money anyway, they gave it to him in New York, and he was very glad to have it.

Education and Choosing a Career

CHAPTER FIVE

Langston had not been back in New York long when he received a letter from his mother. She and Kit were in Washington, D.C., staying with some cousins, and she wanted Langston to join them.

Langston had to think about it awhile. He wasn't sure he wanted to stay with those particular cousins. They were, as Langston put it, the "more high-class branch of the family," direct descendants of Congressman John M. Langston. Langston had always heard that they were rather pretentious and looked down on the rest of the family. He certainly didn't like being around pretentious people.

But he found it hard to say no to his mother. And anyway there really wasn't anything important keeping him in New York. In addition, he had been thinking about returning to college. Dr. Locke taught at Howard University in Washington, D.C.; perhaps he could help him get a scholarship there.

To Langston's great relief his cousins did not treat him like a "poor relation" at all. In fact, at first they treated him as something of a celebrity. They had read his poems and articles in the *Crisis* and seemed pleased to have a poet in residence. Langston hoped the administrators at Howard University would feel the same way. Howard was one of the leading black universities; surely there had to be scholarship money for needy students.

But there was none. Despite the interest of both university officials and Dr. Locke, they could not offer him any financial help. Langston realized that if he was going to go back to college he would have to earn the money for it himself.

He got a job in a laundry sorting dirty clothes, and with his first paycheck he moved from his cousins' home to a furnished room. He was tired of living with relatives, particularly high-class relatives.

Washington, D.C., was a very segregated city. The color line was as strictly drawn as in any city in the deepest South. Not only was there a strict division between white and black, there were also strict divisions among the blacks. The sizable group of monied blacks from good families treated the poorer blacks as cruelly as the whites did, and Langston discovered that the way he was treated depended entirely on whether or not he was recognized as "Langston Hughes, the poet."

Once he attended a dinner at the home of a prominent Washington society woman. The woman seated next to him kept her back to him the entire time. A few days later, Langston received a note from her saying she was sorry she hadn't realized she was sitting next to Langston Hughes, the *poet*, because they could have talked together.

Another time, Washington's leading black literary club held a dinner to honor new black writers. Langston was invited, but he declined, explaining that he had no dinner clothes to wear. The committee wrote back to say he could attend the dinner in whatever clothes he had, and wouldn't he like to bring his mother, too? Under those circumstances, Langston accepted. The day of the dinner his mother got off work early to get ready and was at home when a woman on the committee telephoned. Perhaps it would be better if Langston's mother did not attend the dinner, the woman advised, since it would be a formal affair and Mrs. Clark probably did not have an evening gown. When Langston returned home he found his mother in tears. Of course neither went to the dinner. Langston found this snobbery very tiresome, and after moving out of his relatives' home he rarely returned to the black middle-class section of the city.

Langston was earning only twelve dollars a week, and once he had paid his expenses, there wasn't much left. But he decided to put aside something each week toward college, for he had become determined to get his degree. Unfortunately events would again take a turn to disrupt his plans.

Hardly had Langston gotten settled when his mother joined him. She had suffered some sort of affront from the cousins and pride would not allow her to stay with them any longer. Resigned, Langston found a two-room cold-water flat, and a secondhand oil stove, and gave up the idea of saving for college for a while.

He began to spend a lot of time down on Seventh Street, which was about as far away from his relatives' world as one could get. Lined with honky-tonk bars and soul food restaurants, it was a place where more ordinary black people hung out, where blues songs were played and sung night and day, and where he could feel close to his people. Langston felt comfortable there. He felt good about himself there, too. Usually he would just sit and listen intently to the blues, trying to capture their rhythms in his head to put on paper. It was the closest thing to Harlem outside Harlem.

> *I tried to write poems like the songs they sang on Seventh Street—gay songs, because you had to be gay or die; sad songs, because you couldn't help being sad sometimes. But gay or sad, you kept on living and you kept on going. Their songs—those of Seventh Street—had the pulse beat of people who keep on going.*[12]

Langston kept on going too. When he returned to work from having spent a few days in bed with a cold he found that his job had been given to someone else. After working at a couple of other jobs for a while, he landed a better-paying position as a busboy at the Wardman Park Hotel in downtown Washington. The job included meals. Langston always preferred such jobs, for then he could be assured of eating regularly.

One day Langston grew excited as he read in the newspaper that Vachel Lindsay was coming to the hotel to give a reading of his poems. He had admired Lindsay's poetry since high school. This was a chance he could not pass up. He carefully wrote out three of

Langston working as a busboy in a Washington hotel

his poems, including "The Weary Blues," which he thought especially successful in capturing black musical rhythms, for Lindsay's work was full of musical rhythms. That evening, as Lindsay dined in the hotel restaurant, Langston laid the poems next to his plate, saying he liked Lindsay's poems and here were some of his. Embarrassed, he hurried away before Lindsay could respond.

In the next morning's paper, Langston was surprised to read that Vachel Lindsay had "discovered" a young black poet, who was working as a busboy, and had read some of the young man's poems to the hotel audience the previous night. When he reported for work, he was met by a crowd of reporters and photographers. A picture of Langston dressed in his busboy uniform and carrying a tray of dishes appeared in most of the Washington newspapers. It was the first real publicity he had ever received.

Lindsay had left the hotel but had given the management a set of books for Langston and a note encouraging him to continue writing poetry. A few days later Lindsay and his wife stopped back in Washington, and he and Langston had a brief talk. It was tremendously important to Langston to receive encouragement from a famous poet whom he admired. He would also always be grateful for the publicity Lindsay brought him, although at times he wished he were still unknown. Guests at the hotel were always asking for him, wanting his autograph or his picture, and after a time, when it became too much for the shy Langston, he quit his job.

The Lindsay incident was the beginning of a fruitful time for Langston, a time when he really advanced his career as a poet. Not long after the meeting with Lindsay, Langston entered some of his poems in a literary contest sponsored by *Opportunity*, the official magazine of the National Urban League. One of the poems was "The Weary Blues," and it won first prize.

The prize was cash—forty dollars—and Langston had to spend that much just to travel to New York to accept it. But it was money well-spent, for at the awards' banquet Langston met many writers who were either already famous or would be someday. James Weldon Johnson read "The Weary Blues" to the company. Carl Van Vechten, a well-known white writer with a special interest in black writers, approached Langston and asked him if he had enough poems for a book. Langston said he did, and Van Vechten promised to look them over. If he thought them salable, he would submit them to his publisher, Alfred A. Knopf. Shortly thereafter Langston learned that his work had been accepted for publication, with the title of the volume to be *The Weary Blues.*

Literary doors seemed to open to him unbidden now. He was invited to parties and gatherings where he met other young poets and writers who had converged on Harlem—Zora Neale Hurston, Countee Cullen, Arna Bontemps, Wallace Thurman, Jean Toomer —and where older writers advised and encouraged him. Important magazines began to buy his poems—the first he had ever sold. He won another prize.

It was a time of great excitement for Langston, and he was grateful that all these good things happened when they did. For his life in other aspects was quite unhappy. He was still living in Washington, D.C., with his mother, still troubled by the rampant Jim Crowism of that city, still working at menial, low-paying jobs, and still trying to figure out how to get to college. He had decided Howard University was just too expensive and had set his sights on Lincoln University in Pennsylvania. It was a good school, he had learned, and one could get as fine an education there as at Howard. Still, even though it was less expensive than Howard, Lincoln was far beyond the means of a young black poet, even one who had begun to sell some of his work.

Langston confided his wish to go to college and his financial difficulties to an elderly and wealthy white woman to whom he was introduced in New York. She was very interested in young black writers, who all of a sudden seemed to be coming of age and were gravitating to New York, and she was particularly interested in Langston. At Christmastime in 1925 she wrote to Langston offering him a scholarship to Lincoln. He entered the school at midterm, a twenty-three-year-old freshman.

Lincoln, situated forty miles from Philadelphia in the green rolling hills of Pennsylvania, had an all-black student body and an all-white faculty. Outside of classes there was little contact between the two groups. The students controlled the dormitories and their own campus life. This was fine with the students, who had water-throwing and snowball fights and played all sorts of pranks and practical jokes, as many college students did. Fraternities were very important on campus, and fraternity initiations took up a great deal of Langston's time and patience that first year. Initiations were, of course, intended to make the pledges feel very lowly, and the members of the fraternity to which Langston pledged assumed they would have to work particularly hard on him. After all, he was a published poet who had won prizes and had his name in the papers. Each fraternity brother, afraid that the others were being too soft on Langston, came down doubly hard on him. At no time was this more evident to Langston than at the pledge spanking sessions—after them he couldn't sit down for a week!

As Lincoln was located in the country—the closest large city, Philadelphia, being forty miles away—the students had few outside distractions. They studied hard, but there was time left for reading or for writing poetry, and Langston liked that. He also enjoyed the late-night bull sessions, where the students would gather to talk about things they were learning. But because he missed the excitement of New York he would spend weekends there as often as he could.

It was now the time of the "Harlem Renaissance," when not only black writers but black performers and artists seemed to reach artistic maturity all at the same time in the same place. Of course that wasn't quite true. Black talent had always existed. But the larger society had chosen not to recognize it.

With World War I over, America felt in many ways as if it had come of age. It is hard for us now to understand the feeling in America after the war ended. The idea of a "world war" in the first place was hard for Americans to understand. But when America decided to enter the conflict, it became "the war to end all wars." Our side won, and we were heady with victory. We had shown our military strength, and in the process our industry had developed and boomed. We were a richer country than ever before, we had "arrived" as an industrial nation, and we had matured in our dealings with the rest of the world. But just as maturity in an individual means loss of the innocence and gaiety of youth, so in its maturity did America lose something. At least that was how some

Gaiety in the Harlem nightclubs during the late 1930s

Americans saw it. Phrases such as "The Machine Age" were passed around, and Americans worried that they themselves were being turned into machines or forced into uniformity. They attacked the standardization, the conformity they saw taking place. Many began searching for the qualities they saw receding. And in their search some discovered "the Negro," who to most white Americans in the 1920s was a happy, smiling, dancing, laughing being, untouched by the mechanization affecting white society.

It was the white intelligentsia who did the discovering, and that was understandable. For most of the white intelligentsia were from comfortable backgrounds. They hadn't the slightest inkling of what it was to be black. When they began to seek out blacks in their search for uncorrupted innocence, they naturally met the black intelligentsia—black writers and artists and actors. Confronted with such talent, the whites were happily surprised. But as these blacks were not quite what the whites had expected, a new term was coined to describe them—ironically, it was Dr. Alain Locke who came up with it—the "New Negro."

Before long many whites were traveling up to Harlem to see the New Negro. White entrepreneurs, quick to gauge public taste, opened nightclubs to cater to the whites. These featured black bands, black dancers, and black comedians, many of whom had never before received such exposure. The works of black artists and writers were suddenly in demand; publishing houses and galleries, never interested before, pursued them now.

It was an exhilarating time; talented black people were at last being recognized. And while it must have occurred to most of them that there was nothing "new" about them at all, that they just happened to be in the right place at the right time, they did not want to question it. When you're "in" you don't ask why. You just enjoy it.

Langston, being only a visitor to New York, perhaps had a better perspective about it all. He saw how many blacks tried to conform to the image white people had of them. He saw how Harlem wore two faces—the one presented to white visitors and the one hidden from them.

White people didn't see the poorer Harlemites, those who didn't come to the cafés or nightclubs. They didn't see the resentment that was building against the whites who came to watch them. Some of the smaller clubs which many blacks went to weren't frequented so much by whites. The larger clubs were just showcases—black entertainers with white audiences.

Yet Langston, too, became caught up in the heady atmosphere of the celebration of the New Negro. After all, was he not in college thanks to the generosity of a wealthy white patron? Though he felt he had talent, it must have bothered him at times to be beholden, and he must have occasionally wondered just what might be expected of him in return. Fortunately he was never required to repay in any way the woman who had given him the scholarship.

Langston spent the summer after his first term, the summer of 1926, in New York, where he got to know, among other young black writers, Wallace Thurman. Thurman was managing editor of the *Messenger*, a black magazine, and he bought from Langston the first stories he had ever sold. During that same summer Langston, Thurman, Zora Neale Hurston, and four other young black writers decided to start their own magazine to serve as a forum for the work of the younger black artists and writers. They called it *Fire*, because they intended it to "burn up" many of the ideas of the past. Each of the seven paid—or promised to pay—fifty dollars to finance the magazine. But by the time it went into production, the bills had mounted to almost one thousand dollars, and only three of the seven had even paid the promised fifty.

When the magazine was published, black critics were merciless. "Langston Hughes displays his usual ability to say nothing in many words," observed one article in the *Baltimore Afro-American*.

But the magazine's producers were less worried about criticism than about how to pay the bills. They had hoped to make enough money through sales. However, in a final ironic stroke, most of the copies of *Fire* were burned up in an actual fire! For a long time after, the seven would-be magazine publishers were paying for a publication no longer in existence.

CHAPTER SIX

During his sophomore year at Lincoln, Langston contributed to the college newspaper, took part in intramural track, and gave readings of his poems with the Princeton University Glee Club. He did quite a bit of writing as well. One essay he wrote, "The Negro Artist and the Racial Mountain," was to have an importance not recognized at the time. In it he declared that all writers must explore their own racial "soul world" without regard to the bias of the marketplace. In other words, they should not write only what would sell, but what they felt was true for them. He continued also to write poems and began to choose from among them the best ones for a second volume of poetry. His first volume, *The Weary Blues,* had sold well enough for his publisher, Alfred A. Knopf, to want to publish more of his work.

In the spring of 1927 Langston was invited to read some of his poems both at the commencement of Fisk University, an all-black college in Nashville, Tennessee, and at a YWCA conference in Texas the following week. He accepted eagerly, for except having ridden through on the train to Mexico, he had never actually been to the South.

So Langston spent that summer traveling in the South. While there he was made constantly aware of the strong color bar. During his travels he became so concerned that he would innocently behave in some way Southern blacks were not supposed to that later, looking back on the trip, he felt a little foolish. Particularly embarrassing to him was believing the group of black students he had met at a bus depot. They had told him Southern whites didn't like blacks wearing dark glasses, and he had squinted from the sun for some time before he realized they had been teasing.

Toward the end of the summer Langston found himself in New Orleans. Drawn by an irresistible urge to go to sea again, he signed on as a messboy on a ship traveling to and from Havana, Cuba. He enjoyed himself so much that he would have signed on for another trip if it had not meant missing the first few weeks of school.

Just before he left New Orleans he got together with Zora Neale Hurston, who had also spent the summer traveling in the South, collecting folklore. She was about to start back north, and Langston decided to accompany her. On the way they stopped frequently to visit older black people with stories to tell of slavery days. One old man wore a hat that intrigued Langston. He had to have it. It had been patched so often with leather and linoleum and bits of cloth that the original fabric had long since disappeared. To Langston that hat symbolized the tenacity of everyday black people, their ability to hold on and keep on, no matter what. So he gave the old man his own new straw hat in exchange for the old, battered one.

When he got back to New York Langston took the hat to a Fifth Avenue bank where he rented a safe-deposit box. In the box was an old suitcase containing his most treasured possessions—his manuscripts and his grandmother's shawl. To those he now added that wonderful hat.

The following spring Langston returned once more to his safe-deposit box. It was a Saturday morning, and the vault was crowded with well-dressed people, people who certainly had items of greater value in their boxes than he did in his. His suitcase was handed to him, and when he opened it, to his utter surprise and consternation, a great cloud of moths flew out! They fluttered about and then settled on the expensive clothes and in the well-kept hair of the shocked bank customers. Langston quickly closed the suitcase and left the bank as fast as his feet would carry him. In the privacy of Central Park he opened the suitcase and let the rest of the moths fly out. Of the old hat there remained nothing but a multicolored powder. When Langston returned his suitcase to the safe-deposit box, he did it very early in the morning and would not look at anyone at the bank.

During his junior year at Lincoln, in 1927, Langston's second book of poetry was published. Many poems in it were about ordinary black people, up one day and down the next but always enduring. The very first poem in it, "Hard Luck," was about a man who kept going broke. One day he even had to take his clothes to the pawnshop.

Because blacks called the pawnshop "the Jew's" or "Uncle's," Langston decided to title the book *Fine Clothes to the Jew*. Many Jewish people did not like that at all. Langston felt he had written honestly, but he realized it had been a bad choice of title and wished his publishers had pointed that out to him.

In fact, the book itself was not generally well received by the black press and critics. They criticized Langston for portraying lowly, poor blacks and charged him with creating false images of blacks. Langston understood the reasons for this criticism. No one knew better than he how blacks were usually portrayed in books, stories, and movies—as ignorant, shuffling servants or grinning, laughing clowns. He understood that well-to-do, educated blacks preferred black people to be seen as educated, cultured, and serious. No one wanted to support the stereotypes less than he did, but he did not feel that in writing truthfully about ordinary blacks he was supporting any stereotype. The people about whom he wrote had dignity and individuality of their own. As he later explained, "Certainly, I personally knew very few people anywhere who were wholly beautiful and wholly good. . . . Anyway, I didn't know the upper class Negroes well enough to write much about them. I knew only the people I had grown up with, and they weren't people whose shoes were always shined, who had been to Harvard, or who had heard of Bach. But they seemed to me good people, too." [13]

Ten years later, when social conditions and attitudes had changed, Langston's book would be much better liked by middle-class blacks and would be used at black schools and colleges.

Meanwhile, throughout his years at Lincoln, Langston spent many weekends in New York, for he enjoyed the air of excitement that permeated the artistic and literary community of Harlem. Further, many of his poet and writer friends, not to mention his publishers, were in New York. He attended parties in Harlem that were crowded with famous guests, white and black, European and American. He also went to parties at the homes of white people further downtown.

During one of his weekend visits, Langston was given the name of a very wealthy and distinguished elderly woman who lived on Park Avenue in New York. He subsequently visited Mrs. Mason and found her extremely interested in his work. He told her about his desire to write a novel.

The next time he was in New York, Langston was invited to dine with Mrs. Mason and her family. He accepted but was a bit wary of making some unpardonable mistake in etiquette at the dinner table. The first few courses went smoothly, and by the time dessert was served Langston was more relaxed. Dessert was ice cream with strawberries that still had the caps on. Before eating each strawberry, Langston carefully removed the cap and put it on his plate, so that when he was finished the caps were all that remained. Then he noticed that no one else had caps on their plates. What did rich white folks do with their strawberry caps, he wondered. Was there something he hadn't done that he should have? Finally, Langston could not stand it any longer. What, he asked Mrs. Mason, had the others done with the caps of their strawberries? He had to laugh at himself when he learned that the others, all being allergic to strawberries, hadn't taken any!

Before long Mrs. Mason offered to become his patron and support him while he wrote a novel. Thus, during the summer after his junior year Langston stayed in a dormitory at Lincoln and began to write his first novel, *Not Without Laughter.* It was about a typical black working-class family, a combination of fiction and actual experience.

Langston worked very hard on the novel that summer, taking only a short vacation before classes began again. During his senior year he reworked his novel, though he was very busy with schoolwork, and for a time one project in particular took precedence over the book.

Ever since he had entered Lincoln University, Langston had been disturbed by the lack of black professors. The students were supposedly being trained to be leaders of their race, but Langston felt they were being taught to feel inferior to whites. How could they develop leadership qualities when all their immediate role models were of the race that had oppressed them for so many years? He did not feel it necessary to have all black professors. But to have someone like Dr. Locke on the faculty would show students that black people were just as capable of teaching as white people.

In the senior sociology course, each student had to do a thesis of some sort. Langston chose to do a survey of the Lincoln campus. It would include food, living conditions, academic standards, and so on, but it would also include relations between students and faculty, the area in which Langston was really interested. He wanted to prove his belief that the students were actually being taught to feel inferior.

He interviewed all the juniors and seniors. Sixty-three percent preferred an all-white faculty. Three students said they just did not like blacks. Two said they didn't believe black teachers had the interests of their students at heart. One even said he did not believe members of his race morally capable.

Langston's report concluded, "And the fact that 81 members of the Senior and Junior classes at this college can themselves approve of such a situation, and give reasons for their approval which express open belief in their own inferiority, indicates that the college itself has failed in instilling in these students the very quality of self-reliance and self-respect which any capable American leader should have—and the purpose of this college, let us remember, is to educate 'leaders of the colored people.' "[14]

Needless to say, Langston's survey created quite a furor on campus, and when parts of it were leaked to newspapers and published, a corresponding sensation took place in the black academic world. A number of Southern black elementary and high schools wrote to Lincoln announcing they would no longer hire Lincoln graduates, for they did not want as teachers in their schools people who did not feel blacks were capable of teaching themselves. Within ten years Lincoln would integrate both its faculty and its board of trustees.

Times were changing. A new awareness of the psychological effects of segregation was developing, and it is possible that Lincoln University would have become integrated anyway. But Langston provided the impetus for its beginning. Though he was a quiet, peace-loving young man, he had a strong sense of his own dignity and that of his people. His protest against injustice would never be strident or loudly aggressive. But in his own quiet way he would get results.

CHAPTER SEVEN

At graduation from Lincoln, Langston received not only the diploma for which he had worked more years than he cared to remember, but also the promise of a sizable monthly allowance from Mrs. Mason so that he could continue work on his novel without having to worry about money.

Langston spent most of the summer in a Lincoln dormitory, working on the novel. In the fall he went to New York for a few weeks, to work at a small theater while writing his first play, *Mulatto*. He had wanted to write a play for nearly as long as he had wanted to write stories. His mother had been interested in the stage and had taken him to lots of plays when he was young. And during his year at Columbia he had gradually attended more plays and shows than classes. He enjoyed learning about what went on behind the scenes in a theater and about the particular art of writing plays. Mrs. Mason encouraged him in this project too.

Neither Langston nor Mrs. Mason liked the word "patron," and neither felt theirs was such a formal relationship. Langston really loved this very old, very rich white woman. He admired what she stood for. All her life she had been supporting important movements and causes. Many artists, writers, and humanitarians owed a great deal to her. Once she had been extremely active, but now she was very old and quite feeble and spent most of her time at home. But she was kept informed of the new developments in arts and letters. Her days were filled with answering the letters she received from all over the world and seeing people who came to visit her. In fact, Langston sometimes wondered how she managed or why she cared to find time for him.

For a long time Mrs. Mason had helped blacks by contributing to black schools in the South. When the Harlem Renaissance began, she became interested in black writing. She believed that black people possessed a spirit that was pure and deep—a spirit white people had lost in their commercialism and hunger for money—and that they were America's last link with the primitive. Unless black writers and artists were supported and encouraged, their souls too, she thought, would become polluted.

Sometimes, Mrs. Mason's views bothered Langston a bit. Certainly he believed that black people were pure and deep of spirit. But he disliked the idea that his race was regarded as more primitive than the white. It was the kind of idea held by the whites who patronized the Harlem nightclubs which would not admit blacks except as performers. But other, good feelings obscured these troublesome ones.

All his life Langston had lived with insecurity and fear. Now, for the first time, he had someone who cared for and believed in him and who could provide more than enough money for him to live. She even helped his mother by arranging for his younger brother, Kit, to go to school in New England.

In the fall of 1929 Langston finally finished *Not Without Laughter*, certainly a momentous event in his life. Meanwhile, a momentous event had occurred in the life of the nation. That fall, in October, the stock market crashed. The Great Depression would follow on the heels of the crash, but it didn't come immediately. In New York, some people could not imagine a depression, while others could, but chose not to. Langston was one of those who chose not to.

He was happy and free. For two years he had worked hard on his novel, and now he was written-out. It was a good feeling, rather like the feeling one has after a long hard day of physical labor outdoors. His mind was clear. He was at last free from the characters in the book, whose lives had, over the years, become so important to him. He wanted now to have some fun, to go to parties and plays and shows.

Mrs. Mason's generosity made it possible for him to do so, and in style. No matter what the show, her secretary could get him tickets to it. Clothing? He could use her charge accounts at all the major stores. And sometimes he even had the use of her limousine and chauffeur.

One day that winter Langston attended a luncheon with Mrs. Mason. Having stayed longer than intended, he realized he would have to rush to catch the train that would take him to the first stop on a midwinter lecture trip. Afraid that he would not get to the train station in time by taxi, Mrs. Mason ordered her chauffeur to take Langston to the station and sent her secretary along to purchase his tickets while he had his baggage checked.

The long town-car whizzed through downtown traffic to Pennsylvania Station and drew up to the ramp on which a dozen porters were waiting to greet the cars and take the baggage. As Langston emerged from the car with Mrs. Mason's secretary, he recognized a number of the porters as young men with whom he had gone to college. Like many other young educated blacks of the time, they had been unable to get professional work. There were only so many black schools to hire black teachers, and black doctors and lawyers fared little better than James Hughes had twenty-five-odd years before. Needless to say, they were quite impressed to see Langston get out of a limousine driven by a white chauffeur and accompanied by a white secretary.

As winter wore on, evidence of the depression became more and more visible. Unemployment numbers increased drastically, as did the number of ragged figures begging for food or small change on the streets. Harlem was hit first and hardest, and gradually the gaiety of the Harlem Renaissance disappeared. The resentment of the common Harlemites, hidden earlier by the glitter of "the New Negro," became ominously apparent. Whites, worried more and more about money, stopped traveling north to

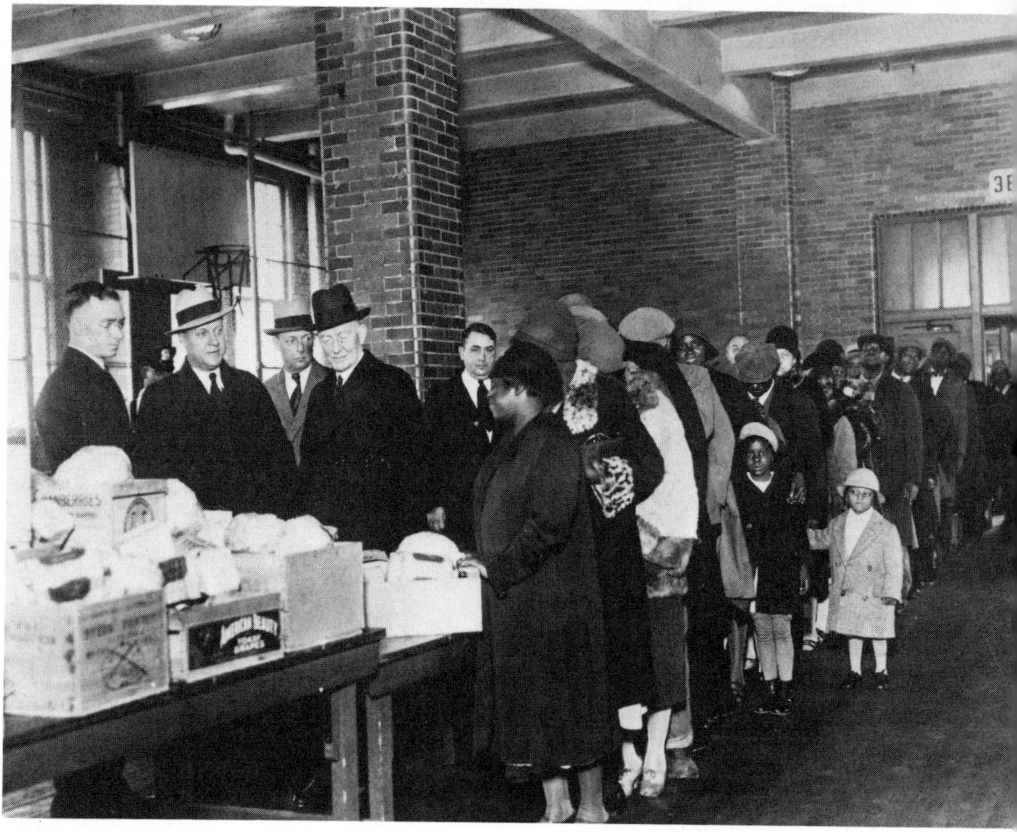

Poverty and hunger of the Harlem unemployed during the Great Depression

the whites-only clubs. Before long the Harlem Renaissance was over.

The end came as a very unpleasant surprise to some, but not to Langston. Perhaps his childhood experiences with poverty and discrimination had given a clearer picture of American society to him than to those blacks who had grown up in more comfortable circumstances.

"I was there," he would later recall, meaning in Harlem during the Renaissance. "I had a swell time while it lasted. But I thought it wouldn't last long. . . . For how could a large and enthusiastic number of people be crazy about Negroes forever?" [15]

But more than just loss of black popularity was involved in the white exodus from Harlem. Harlem economic life suffered as well. When the whites stopped coming, the clubs that had catered to them closed, and a lot of Harlemites who had worked in the clubs joined the already large numbers of Harlem unemployed. Langston felt bad for them, and he began to feel guilty about buying new clothes and riding around in a chauffeur-driven limousine. He also felt guilty when he thought of his mother's working as a cook in a rest home in Atlantic City, New Jersey, or of his relatives in Cleveland who were struggling. Here he was, living in luxury but doing nothing for a living. Why he wasn't even writing.

For two years he had worked on a novel, some poems, and a play. The effort had left him mentally and emotionally spent, and he had not written a thing for months. Besides, he really had nothing to write about. So far he had written only when he was unhappy or when he had something very important to say. In New York that winter he was happy and contented, and in his novel he had said everything important that he wanted to say for a time. Without an inner need to write, he just didn't feel like writing. But Mrs. Mason did not seem to understand this.

As the winter wore on, she became more and more impatient with him. Each time he visited her, she asked if he was writing and why not and when was he going to start. "I didn't realize," he would write later, "that she was old and wanted quickly to see my books come into being before she had to go away. She hadn't told me that I must always write and write. . . ." [16]

Langston began to feel pressured. He remembered his father and those months in Mexico when all he seemed to hear was "Hurry up," as he struggled over bookkeeping problems. Of course Mrs. Mason was not like his father, and he wanted so to please her. He was almost relieved when an idea for a poem came to him. The Waldorf Astoria, a huge luxury hotel, opened on Park Avenue that spring. Langston wrote a poem about the irony of such a monument to wealth opening in the midst of a depression, offering luxurious suites while homeless people were sleeping under newspapers in Grand Central Station, charging outrageous prices for its dinners when hungry people stood in soup lines for a free meal. He thought it was a pretty good poem, but when he showed it to Mrs. Mason he could tell immediately she didn't like it. "It isn't you," she said.

Langston thought that a strange comment. He had written it, hadn't he? But he realized that what she wanted him to write was not social commentary but rhythmic, primal poems, and stories about simple, happy blacks in whom the primitiveness of Africa was still alive. Sadly, Langston realized that Mrs. Mason did not know *him* at all. He could not write what she wanted him to write. What's more, as he had expressed in "The Negro Artist and the Racial Mountain," he would not. Knowing this he could no longer accept her money.

So one early spring morning Langston went to the Park Avenue apartment to explain his feelings to his patron. He could not take any more of her money, he told her, or accept any more of her help; but he wanted very much to remain her friend. Mrs. Mason did not understand at all. She considered him ungrateful. As her voice droned on and on in the large, sunlit room, Langston began not to hear what she was saying. He knew only that he had been wrong about her, that she had cared not about him but only about what he wrote. He saw her as if through a haze; his head began to spin. When he found himself on the street again he could not remember how he had gotten there, and he did not know how he was going to make it home, for his stomach was turning over and over, just as it had that morning of the trip to Mexico City years before.

He went to a doctor that day, and in succeeding weeks to other doctors. Though he was diagnosed in various ways, he knew that his illness was really caused by violent emotion turned inward upon himself. Finally, he returned home to Cleveland and to bed.

Langston's mother and Homer Clark were living in three furnished rooms in Cleveland with Kit, who had left school in New England in order to get a job to help out at home. Lying in bed, looking at the shabby furnished room, listening to the family's worried talk about money, Langston despaired. It seemed to him that they were right back where they had started—unsettled, not even knowing whether they would have enough to eat the next day. He had been far away from them both geographically and in terms of experience; he had been to college and graduated. Yet here he was, dependent on them again. He was so unhappy that had he felt well enough he could have written a book of poems.

Several weeks later, however, he was lifted out of his despair quite as quickly as he had been plunged into it. *Not Without Laughter*, which had been published in the spring, won the Harmon Gold Award for Literature. The award was a gold medal and four hundred dollars, which, because he was too sick to accept his prize in person, had to be mailed to him.

The actual prize was not what mattered to Langston. More important was the confidence that winning the award gave him. Though he had been writing for years he had never actually thought of making his living as a writer. He had always held menial jobs or received money from a patron. Now he determined that he would not only continue to write, but he would try to make his living at it. He felt so good about this decision that his stomach pains disappeared almost immediately.

Out of bed and feeling healthy again, Langston decided to delay writing for a living a little longer. He had four hundred dollars, the most money he had ever had at one time. First he would take a vacation. He felt he needed some sun.

Mary McLeod Bethune

Always Movin' On

CHAPTER EIGHT

Langston decided to go to Cuba and Haiti. His original plan was to go alone, but while he was still in Cleveland he had become friendly with Zell Ingraham, a young, discontented art student who wanted to go with him. So with Zell's mother's car and an additional $300 Zell had gotten from his mother, the two set out for Miami. They stopped along the way in Daytona Beach, Florida, to visit Mary McLeod Bethune, president of Bethune-Cookman College and America's best-known black woman. Langston had met Mrs. Bethune at Columbia, and of course she knew his poems. In Miami they left the car and took a boat to Cuba, where Langston, who had been to Cuba two summers before, enjoyed showing Zell around.

From Cuba the two went to Haiti. Langston had brought letters of introduction from influential American artists and writers, letters that would have allowed him to meet important Haitians. But since he felt he did not have enough money to socialize with the upper-class Haitians, he did not use the letters. Instead, he and Zell stayed with the lower classes, listening to fishermen's stories and attending their celebrations and funerals. Class and color lines, they found, were very rigid in this black-governed country—a sad situation in a country whose black inhabitants had in the nineteenth century revolted against their white colonial masters and established an independent black republic. Haiti reminded him of Washington, D.C., where blacks discriminated against each other on the basis of color and class. Most Haitians were so poor they owned neither coats nor shoes. To distinguish themselves as being of a better class, those who did own coats or shoes made sure never to be seen in public without them. Langston thought it funny to see men suffering in the hot tropical climate because they were too class-conscious to shed their coats.

Langston spent much time with the common people, those who owned neither coats nor shoes, because he found them much more interesting. So he walked around coatless and barefoot and sat on the ground as he talked to fishermen as they repaired their nets. At the port city of Cap Haitien, where the revolution for independence had begun, Langston's hotel manager was mortified that a man of Langston's class would behave in such a manner. Try as he might Langston simply could not make the man understand his feelings.

By the time they were ready to leave Haiti, Langston and Zell had very little money left. They had to take passage on a Dutch boat as deck passengers with no accommodations—not even food and shelter. The boat stopped for a day at Port-au-Prince, Haiti, where Langston made a brief visit to the home of the well-known writer Jacques Roumain. Then he rejoined Zell at the boat. Since it was very hot, they stripped off their shirts and socks before beginning to eat their meal of bread, cheese, and wine.

Just then the captain escorted to their corner of the deck a delegation of Haitian writers and government officials dressed in tailcoats and gloves. One writer, unhappy that Langston had not given him a chance to extend his hospitality, had arranged a formal farewell! Langston never found out what that delegation of leading Haitians thought of his riding as a deck passenger, like any commoner, and greeting them without shirt or socks!

Langston and Zell had stayed in Haiti much longer than they had originally intended. By the time they returned to Miami to reclaim Zell's mother's car it was not in running order. Repairs took all their remaining money, and Miami was a long, long way from their intended destination, New York. Langston had about thirty dollars in a bank account in New York, but no one in Miami would cash his check. Just when he and Zell were about to despair, Langston remembered Mrs. Bethune. He was sure her college would cash his check.

They drove to Daytona Beach, and, sure enough, Mrs. Bethune cashed his check for him. She decided, furthermore, that it was time she visited New York again. She could save carfare by riding up with Langston and Zell. Now Mrs. Bethune was a very large woman, and Zell's was a very small car with only one seat. Langston and Zell groaned at the thought of riding hundreds of miles squeezed like sardines into that one small seat with Mrs. Bethune, but they could not say no.

By the end of the trip, they were delighted they hadn't. The only thing they had had to pay for during the whole trip was gasoline. Mrs. Bethune had friends all along the way, who laid out delicious feasts for them and provided comfortable beds and enjoyable entertainment.

Such hospitality on the part of Southern blacks to other blacks passing through, however, was not merely generosity—it was necessity. Jim Crow reigned in the South, and restaurants that would serve or hotels that would accommodate blacks were few and far between. Blacks traveling through avoided as much as possible the segregation to which they were subjected, but sometimes it was impossible to. There were times, for instance, when it was necessary to stop at a service station to use the restroom. In those days there were three types of restrooms at Southern service stations. One was marked MEN, one was marked LADIES, and one was marked COLORED. This last was usually a shack in the bushes way out back. As well-known and dignified-looking as she was, Mrs. Bethune was forced to use those facilities if any white customers were around the service stations.

When Langston arrived back in New York the effects of the depression were much more evident than when he had left. Bread lines were longer, beggars and peddlers on the streets were more numerous, and more of his friends and acquaintances had lost their jobs. Langston was very glad *he* was not looking for a job, for he knew he would have had a hard time getting one. There were hardly any job opportunities for black writers. Some white writers he knew had jobs on the staffs of magazines or with book publishers, but blacks could not get such jobs. Magazines might occasionally publish stories about blacks, but they were considered "special interest" stories, in the same category with stories about Orientals or Indians. Magazine and book publishers never even thought of having blacks on their staffs. In Hollywood, white writers were hired to do movie scripts. Others wrote radio scripts. But while these writers' works received nowhere near as fine reviews as Langston's had, they held jobs for which he could never even be considered. So Langston had to figure out another way to make money through his writing.

One day he remembered a suggestion Mrs. Bethune had made, that he should take his poetry to the black colleges in the South. The students needed to hear poetry about black people by a black poet. Langston had gone on speaking trips before and had been paid for them, so he decided to explore that source of income. Not only would he be making money but he would also be taking his poetry to the people for whom it was really intended.

In the following weeks Langston wrote to the presidents of all the Southern colleges, offering his services. He received many invitations and expressions of interest; the only trouble was, most could offer him only small honorariums. There was simply no money for travel expenses. Langston decided to try to get a foundation grant to finance his trip. He wrote to the Rosenwald Fund to Aid Negro Education, and to his delight he was awarded a one-thousand-dollar grant.

But even the thousand dollars would not cover all his travel expenses if he took buses and trains. So he bought a car. With a former classmate of his at Lincoln, Radcliffe Lucas, who was willing to leave his job as a redcap at Pennsylvania Station to be his driver, Langston set out in September.

The tour was very successful; despite the depression Langston sold a number of his books. It was his first really long trip through the South. He found great hospitality at the black colleges, but he also found many disappointing things. The heads of the colleges were strangely silent about contemporary problems. While he was at Hampton University in Virginia the news arrived that the Dean of Women at Fisk University had died because she had been denied admission to a whites-only hospital. About the same time one of Hampton's football stars was beaten to death by a mob of whites after he had mistakenly parked his car in a white parking lot. The Hampton students were naturally angry and upset over these incidents. They wanted to hold a protest meeting, but the university officials forbade it. Their slogan was, "We educate, not protest."

Langston was saddened by this experience. He had thought the problem at Lincoln was that black students could not be taught to be leaders by white professors and administrators. He realized, now, that the *attitude* of the professors and administrators was the most important consideration. Institutions like Hampton, with both white and black teachers, had been born out of the abolitionist spirit of the Civil War and Reconstruction—a proud spirit. But it seemed to Langston that this spirit had been replaced over the years by a conservatism born of fear.

What especially disturbed Langston was the lack of protest on behalf of the Scottsboro boys, nine black teen-agers accused of raping two white prostitutes in a railroad car. The boys were on trial for their lives in Alabama. Most blacks, and many whites, did not believe the prostitutes' story, and Langston felt the teen-agers were being "railroaded" to conviction. He felt so strongly about the injustice of the case that he wrote several poems about it.

While most of Langston's engagements were at black schools, some were at white schools. In November he was scheduled to be at the University of North Carolina in Chapel Hill. A week before his appearance he received a note from a white student advising him that since a black would not be allowed to stay on campus Langston could stay with him and his roommate. The two students ran a small bookstore off campus and published a newspaper considered radical. They asked Langston to contribute

The Scottsboro boys with their lawyer, 1933

something to the newspaper that would announce his coming. Langston sent a poem and an article, both about the Scottsboro case.

These created quite a commotion. When Langston arrived to speak, the hall was filled to overflowing. In fact some people had reacted to the poem and article so angrily that there was fear for his life and Langston found himself with official police protection. Moreover, because they had published the material, the two students were evicted from their lodgings, and Langston ended up staying with a black family.

But the students insisted on taking him to dinner. Together with some fellow white students they went to a downtown, segregated restaurant. Langston was most uncomfortable about going to the restaurant, for in all likelihood he would not be served. Further, he was not sure what the students would do if this happened. But to his astonishment—and to many others' as well —he was served!

However, Langston did not feel particularly elated over his triumph. He had been very nervous and uncomfortable. Such aggressive behavior was just not his style.

There were other times on his trip through the South when he and Radcliffe Lucas were subjected to indignities. Once, when they stopped at a roadside stand to buy soft drinks to take out, they were served through a hole in the outside wall of the structure. Another time, when Langston went into the WHITE waiting room of a railroad station to buy a newspaper, he was stopped by a policeman, who refused to let him go out the door facing the street. That door, the policeman explained, was for the use of whites. But he had just entered through the same door, Langston protested. No matter, said the policeman. Langston had to leave by way of the railroad tracks on the other side of the station.

Most of the time, however, they avoided such situations. They spent their nights and ate most of their meals in the homes of blacks along the way, who showed them great hospitality. They ate until they were stuffed and were entertained until they dropped.

One woman, for instance, in preparation for his visit, had cleaned her entire house from top to bottom and painted all the woodwork with fresh white paint. Regrettably, however, at the last minute she also decided to paint the bathtub, inside and out. When Langston arrived, tired and hot, he decided to take a nice, hot bath. He settled into the tub and soaped up. Ten minutes later, thoroughly refreshed, he started to get up. But to his surprise he could not move. He was completely stuck to the bottom of the tub! Eventually he managed to pry himself loose without losing any skin. But when the soapy water drained out of the tub, he discovered he had left what he called "his most personal autograph!"

Langston traveled to every state in the South. In Alabama he visited the Scottsboro boys, but he felt very much at a loss as to what to say to them. What could one say to nine teen-agers on trial for their lives? He tried to cheer them up by reading his most humorous poems but generally failed. It was almost Christmas then.

His last program of the year was near Huntsville, Alabama, where one of the white women the boys were accused of raping lived. She had dropped charges against the boys, yet they were still in jail. Langston wanted to interview her, but no one from Oakwood Junior College, where he was speaking, would accompany him to see her. He finally gave up the idea for fear of causing trouble to the college. But the Scottsboro case continued to command his attention. At every appearance he read at least one poem about it.

Finally Langston reached California. There he met a wealthy white couple, the Sullivans, who were very interested in his work. They were so hospitable and so eager to make him feel comfortable that they even offered him the services of their secretary.

While in California, Langston received a telegram from New York inviting him to join a black motion picture group being organized in Harlem to go to Russia. There they would make a film on race and labor relations in the United States. Fifteen years before, Russia had experienced a revolution during which the wealthy classes and nobility had been overthrown by the working classes. The "New Russia" was a socialist state: the state owned all property and all people were supposedly equal. Russia, claiming to be the champion of oppressed peoples everywhere, was particularly interested in the black people of the United States. Langston was invited to do the English dialogue of the film on a four-month contract. He drove back to New York as fast as he could, packed his clothes, his phonograph, and his favorite records—Louis Armstrong, Bessie Smith, Duke Ellington, and Ethel Waters—and just made the ship for Moscow.

CHAPTER NINE

On arriving in Moscow, the group were settled into the luxurious Grand Hotel in the center of the city. Since it would be a month before the scenario of the film, which was being written by the Russians, would be finished, they were free to enjoy the city, with all expenses paid. Langston found the people there more polite to strangers, particularly black American strangers, than any other people he'd ever met. But he was aware of the Russian interest in American blacks and knew that the Scottsboro case had received worldwide publicity.

At last the scenario, or script, for the film was finished. But when it was translated for Langston he nearly burst out laughing. The Russian writer had never been to America, and only a few books on contemporary black American life had been translated into Russian. Thus, nearly every page contained some gross error about American life or about black–white relations. Anyone familiar with America who saw the film according to that scenario would think it a comedy!

Naturally the Russian filmmakers were distressed to learn the script was not true to life. They asked Langston to rewrite it, but he declined. He explained that he had never lived in the South or worked in a steel mill, and he knew very little about unions or race relations. He knew only that the script was not true to life, not how to correct it.

While the scenario was being rewritten, the group continued

to enjoy Moscow with all expenses paid. They were even invited on a pleasure cruise of the Black Sea. While on the cruise, they learned from newspapers that their movie, *Black and White,* had been abandoned. Although they had been paid well and had had a good time, many in the group were angry. They charged that the film had been abandoned because of pressure from the American government. Langston was not particularly angry. He did not see how anything meaningful could have been written by people who did not understand the race problem in America anyway.

Some of the group went home immediately. Others, who accepted an invitation by the Russians to travel in the country, wanted particularly to see those areas where most of the nonwhite citizens lived—the Turkmen Republic and Soviet Central Asia. Their Russian hosts were hesitant about granting this request, for these areas were off limits to foreigners.

Far from Moscow geographically, these areas were equally far removed from the customs and ways of life in Moscow. Before the Revolution, nonwhites had been segregated in Jim Crow cars and other public places, just as blacks were in the Southern United States. The women were even required to wear veils. Men could buy wives, and a wealthy man could have many wives. Many of the areas were dusty and infertile, the people there living in poverty and filth. Since the Revolution, such customs as segregation of nonwhites and wife buying had been outlawed, and much had been done to raise economic and health standards and to make educational and cultural reforms. But the areas were not yet "sovietized," or ready for very close inspection by visitors, particularly foreign visitors. But Langston's group would not be talked out of it, and Langston even applied for a press permit so he could remain in Soviet Central Asia long enough to write about it for publication in America. Finally permission was granted.

It was like traveling through another world. The peoples' dress, their customs, their languages were unlike anything they had ever experienced before. One evening they arrived in Tashkent, the regional center of Soviet Asia. As the train pulled into the station, Langston looked out at the crowd of Asiatic artists, writers, and actors who had come to meet them. Right there on the station platform was a young American black, dressed in of all things a tuxedo! A graduate of the Department of Engineering at Howard University in Washington, D.C., the young man was in Soviet Asia helping to bring modern conveniences to the people. "Having since been around the world," Langston remarked, "I have learned that there is at least *one* Negro everywhere."

Everywhere the group went they were greeted by official delegations and shown only selected sites where sovietization had been accomplished. Langston was bored with this kind of touring. He decided that after the group visited Ashkhabad he would remain there while the rest went on. That way he could see what it was really like to live in Soviet Central Asia.

By the time they reached Ashkhabad, the rest of the group had decided not to visit the city after all. Langston was angry, because he had counted on their interpreter's helping him get settled. He knew no one there and was to learn that there was at that time not one single person in Ashkhabad who spoke English. Soon, however, he discovered he had something that worked just as well as words—his Louis Armstrong records!

Upon leaving the train, Langston went straight to the nearest hotel and rented a room. He still felt angry at his Russian guides for abandoning him. Further, he felt lonely, depressed, and a little homesick. It occurred to him that he might feel better if he played some good American jazz. So he set up his phonograph and put on a Louis Armstrong record. Soon there came a knock on the door. A young Ashkhabadian grinned at Langston and made straight for the phonograph. They conversed with smiles and sign language. Soon Langston had his first friend—thanks to Louis Armstrong.

Langston would find the same thing wherever he went: "Everywhere, around the world, folks are attracted by American jazz. A good old Dixieland stomp can break down almost any language barriers, and there is something about Louis Armstrong's horn that creates spontaneous friendships." [17]

It was Langston's jazz records that also first brought Langston and German writer Arthur Koestler together. Koestler arrived in

Ashkhabad a few days after Langston and checked in at the same hotel. Hearing the sounds of American jazz, he knocked on the door and introduced himself—in English! Langston was very happy to see him. The two traveled together from then on. Later, through such books as *Darkness at Noon* and *The Invisible Writing,* Koestler would become world famous.

Langston added another part of the world to his reading audience during his stay in Soviet Asia. The State Publishers of Uzbekistan in Soviet Central Asia bought his book, *The Weary Blues,* for translation. His poems would now be read in places like Samarkand and Bukhara, Kokand and Fergana.

In Ashkhabad and the surrounding area, Langston saw amazing poverty and squalor. The countryside, where state-owned farms had been set up, was a barren and ugly desert. Far out in the desert he visited people who were reported to be so wild that they would kill any stranger. There he saw such filth and disease he could not believe his eyes. Yet in Ashkhabad he saw nonwhite students being taught motion-picture skills denied to blacks in the United States. And, amazingly, in the middle of barren desert he saw leafy, green oases inhabited by nonwhite people who seemed to belong to another time. There were beautiful women in tall, hollow, cone hats covered with bright silks and coins, and men in high, black, shaggy hats, some with fierce-looking mustaches. Cotton was grown in these oases. It was a strange combination of old and new, this home of the nonwhite citizens of Russia.

During his stay in Soviet Asia, Langston had stomach trouble again, although this time it was due not to emotional upset but to diet. For weeks he had eaten camel meat, tough camel sausage, and bread as hard as a rock, and finally it all seemed to come together in a big lump in the pit of his stomach. The first doctor who treated him did not speak English. Obviously he did not understand Langston's explanation of what was wrong. The bright green liquid he prescribed made Langston sicker than he had ever been in his life. Later he learned that the doctor had thought the trouble was not with Langston's stomach but with his heart. The bright green liquid Langston had been taking was arsenic!

Early in the spring Langston returned to Moscow and immediately became tangled in red tape. All his various permits had been issued for a six-month period. He had now been in Russia six months and two days. His residence permit had expired, so he could not get a hotel room. His food card had expired, so he could not get any food. He had plenty of money, but without the permits the money was just worthless paper. To make matters even worse, Langston realized his American passport was about to expire. He had reached, as he later put it, his "zero hour."

Luckily he was invited to stay with the editor of an English-language magazine, who used his influence to help Langston get his papers renewed.

The incredible amount of red tape—papers, permits, cards—was one of the things most Americans in Russia hated about the country. Many had come expecting to find a land of equality and prosperity. Most of them were soon disillusioned by the realities of Soviet life; not only by the endless red tape but by the scarcity of food and the disorganized system of production. Instead of the paradise they had expected to find, they discovered a struggling, impoverished land.

Besides the difficulty in getting his various papers and permits renewed, Langston experienced his share of other frustrations, if not all so serious, under the Soviet system. Russian food stores, for instance, did not supply paper bags, or even paper with which to wrap food. Customers had to bring their own baskets and their own paper.

One day, after he had returned to Moscow, Langston passed by a foreign food store. Seeing that French bread was available that day, he decided to buy a loaf. Of course the clerk handed him the loaf of bread without any wrapping. It was snowing outside, and Langston did not want the bread to get wet. He asked for some paper. The clerk refused. He went to the manager. He, too, said Langston could not have any paper. Angrily, Langston informed the manager that he would sit right there in the office until he got some.

Half an hour later, realizing Langston was not going to go away, the manager gave him a few inches of brown wrapping paper.

It was only enough to cover the middle of the loaf, but Langston knew he would never get any more and finally gave up and left.

But despite such frustrations and inconveniences, Langston decided that the good in Soviet Russia outweighed the bad. Most important to him was the total lack of segregation. In his mind, the Soviet Union scored many points on that alone.

Now back in Moscow, Langston began to think again about writing. Marie Seaton, an English writer, was staying in the same hotel as Langston. She lent him a book of short stories by D. H. Lawrence, entitled *The Lovely Lady*. He was greatly impressed by the stories; the characters seemed so very alive and the plots so powerful. He thought about some of the people he had known in his own life and some of the true stories he'd heard. He had now had four books of poems published, including two small volumes, *Dear Lovely Death* (1931) and *The Dream Keeper* (1932), the latter of which had been published in the United States while he was in Russia. He had also had a novel published and written quite a few articles. But though he had wanted to write stories ever since he had read those of Guy de Maupassant back in high school, he had written very few. Now, he decided, it was time to become a short-story writer as well as a poet.

The first few he wrote were about the relationship between a young artist and his patron. Lawrence's story, "Lovely Lady," about an extremely possessive elderly woman had reminded Langston of Mrs. Mason. He sent the stories to an agent in New York, and by the time he returned to America they had been sold to three well-known magazines. Knowing his stories were good, he now wrote one after another—about people he'd known and people he'd heard about. Sometimes he would transform a story he had heard into something of his own, just as he had done with the first blues verse he had ever heard when writing "The Weary Blues." All through the spring he wrote—and not just short stories but articles about his trip through Central Asia as well. He sold several of these articles to Russian magazines. As he was paid very well for them he decided to return to the United States by way of Japan and China.

It took three months for him to get clearance, the necessary papers, and a compartment on the Trans-Siberian Railroad. When all the arrangements had finally been made he could hardly believe it. Immediately he started giving away his belongings and the souvenirs he had collected in Russia, for he wanted to travel light. He kept his phonograph and Louis Armstrong records, of course, but gave away his books, his soap, even his camera. To his dismay, however, he received so many farewell presents from friends he had made in Moscow that he was no better off than when he had started!

CHAPTER TEN

Langston rode the train for ten days to reach Vladivostok, where he boarded a boat for Japan.

Upon their arrival in Japan, all the boat's passengers were questioned by the police, who wanted to know why they had been in Russia, how long, and why they had stayed as long as they had. Russia and Japan were not on good terms. The police were suspicious of anyone who traveled to Japan by way of Russia.

In Japan, Langston at first went largely unrecognized. He was happy to be able to explore the country by himself without being obliged to give interviews or attend official functions. But in Tokyo, only a few days after he arrived, he was visited by a delegation of Japanese writers, actors, artists, and journalists, who had somehow learned of his arrival and were eager to show him hospitality. For the next two weeks he was interviewed and photographed and escorted about town. But while he appreciated his hosts' efforts, he wished he had not been discovered. Langston was never very comfortable being the center of attention. He preferred to be on the sidelines, watching, trying to decide what made people behave as they did.

During his stay in Tokyo he was asked to be guest speaker at the monthly luncheon of the Pan Pacific Club, a club with both Japanese and foreign members. He was seated next to a white woman from St. Louis, the wife of an American official. The two times Langston had been in St. Louis, he had been refused service in downtown restaurants. He thought it ironic that he should be dining at the same table with her here. In his speech he pointed out that irony and praised Japan, saying he hoped the country would not become race conscious as it became more westernized. As most of the people in the room were nonwhite, he was heartily applauded. But the American woman reproached him for not speaking very well of his country.

After leaving Tokyo and Japan, Langston traveled to Shanghai in China. Like Tokyo it was a free port, where people of many nationalities lived and did business. Because western commercial influence was strong there, color lines were quite strict in some parts of the city. In the International Settlement, where the whites lived, none of the leading hotels would accept black or Asiatic guests. Langston was amazed that white foreigners could so casually discriminate against the Chinese in their own country.

Shanghai was full of crime and corruption. The narcotics trade flourished, beggars were everywhere, and kidnapping seemed a major business. Langston was warned by other Americans not to go far from the International Settlement, especially at night, but he did not take the warnings seriously. He found the Chinese in Shanghai very friendly and compared their jolly manner with that of black people in the United States.

Many black performers were in Shanghai. Langston never ceased to be amazed how worldwide were American blacks and their music. He had found the same true of Japan; the blues and jazz were very popular there.

Shanghai was a very expensive city. Langston's money soon ran so low that he had to cable his publisher, Alfred A. Knopf, in New York, for an advance on his royalties. With the money he bought a ticket on the *Taiyo Maru*, sailing for San Francisco by way of Yokohama, Japan.

Before reaching Yokohama the *Taiyo Maru* stopped for a day at Kobe, Japan, to load cargo, and the passengers were allowed to go ashore. As they stepped off the gangplank, all passengers were required to go through a routine check of their papers by Japanese officials. But when Langston's turn came, not only did he have to show his papers, but he was also questioned: Why did you go to China? Who did you see there? Langston thought it strange that he had been singled out for questioning. Again at Yokohama, he was the only passenger questioned.

Since the ship was not scheduled to leave Yokohama for three days, Langston decided to spend the time in Tokyo. But he did not get to enjoy those three days very much. The morning after he arrived he was summoned to the police station and questioned all day. The police assured him he was not under arrest; yet they would not let him keep a luncheon appointment with a group of Japanese writers. He soon learned that the Japanese were very suspicious about the purpose of his trip to Japan by way of Russia and of his visit to China. Japan was not on friendly terms with either country, and Langston's interrogators suspected that he had been carrying messages and perhaps had secret documents from Russia and China for the communists in Japan. They even had a complete file on all his activities in Shanghai and Tokyo. If it hadn't been such a serious matter, Langston would have found the whole situation funny. He a spy? The closest he had ever been to international intrigue was when he sat in movie theaters watching spy movies.

Finally the Japanese officials finished their questioning and politely informed Langston that he should leave Japan as soon as possible and not return. Langston, tired of answering all their questions and annoyed at having been kept a virtual prisoner all day, retorted sharply that he did not travel around the world every year and did not expect to return again soon.

As he left the police station Langston realized that the Japanese authorities were still not convinced he was just a harmless American tourist—either that, or they had decided not to take any chances. Two stout men were just behind him as he walked along the busy Tokyo streets. He realized they must be plainclothes detectives. He thought of hailing a taxi and trying to lose them, but he really didn't have enough money to spend on taxis. So instead he quickened his pace and got great pleasure from watching the two out-of-condition detectives huffing and puffing in their efforts to keep up with him. After a while, the two detectives decided it was easier to pay the cab fare for all three of them rather than have to follow Langston on foot. So Langston got to see a lot more of Tokyo than he would have if he had had to walk, and the two detectives proved to be quite friendly.

Back aboard the *Taiyo Maru* and later in Hawaii, Langston read many newspaper reports of his experience with the Japanese police, most of which were false. A number of articles mentioned an interview he was supposed to have given. In it he was quoted as saying Japan would be the saviour of the darker peoples of the world and praising Japan's pro-war and imperialist attitudes. These false reports angered Langston, but he dismissed them as unimportant. He had no way of knowing that in 1941 Japanese planes would bomb the American fleet at Pearl Harbor, Hawaii. He also could not foresee that in the future in the United States anyone who had visited Soviet Russia would be suspected of being communist.

CHAPTER ELEVEN

The voyage back to the United States by way of the Pacific Ocean was long, rough, and uncomfortable. Langston was relieved to see the gleaming arches of the Golden Gate Bridge and awfully glad to be back in his own country again. Earlier he had written to Noel Sullivan announcing his return and telling him he wanted to do nothing but sit around and write short stories for a while. Sullivan, in response, had graciously offered the use of his cottage at Carmel-by-the-Sea. Thus, soon after arriving, Langston settled into the cottage, with the Sullivans' German shepherd, Greta, for company, and a Filipino houseboy. He felt himself lucky to have a cozy, quiet place to write, far away from Harlem and the miserable effects of the Great Depression. It would be the longest stretch of time he had ever had to just write and worry about little else.

Carmel was a prosperous and socially conscious community. It was also the home of a number of well-known people. With some of the community's other writers and artists, Langston engaged in many charitable activities, including an auction of paintings and drawings by famous artists for the benefit of the Scottsboro boys. The Scottsboro case would, in fact, continue to drag on through numerous trials, appeals, and retrials. In 1936–37 four of the boys were convicted and sentenced to prison terms. The other five were freed. The case would go down as one of the most sensational in U.S. history. Langston also participated in a fund-raising drive to aid the migrant laborers who had come to California to work on the farms and were nearly starving because of the low wages. But most of the time he just wrote—sometimes ten or twelve hours a day—producing at least one story a week. Magazines bought every one. Later, most of these stories would be combined in a volume entitled *The Ways of White Folks.* He also wrote several articles. One about the liberation of women in Soviet Asia brought the highest fee he had ever received. But he sent most of his earnings to his mother, who had written him that fall that she was not well and did not know where her husband was.

In late summer, 1934, Langston was invited to Reno, Nevada, for a weekend. Since he decided to stay when the weekend was over, he moved to a room in the black section of the very segregated city. Every afternoon, by which time he had already put in several hours of writing, he would take a long walk; one November day he found himself on a dusty road that led out of the city. At one point he saw ahead of him a tiny cemetery on a hill. As he drew nearer he was startled to see on the cemetery's weather-beaten gate what looked like a mailbox. A mailbox for the dead? he asked himself. But as he approached the gate he realized that it was only one of the boards on the old gate, which had warped into the shape of a mailbox. Nevertheless he thought "Mailbox for the Dead" a very good title for a story and began to think about a situation to fit the title. That evening, as he sat writing, he thought of his father, which was a bit strange. He did not think of his father often. He had not seen him in thirteen years—since the unhappy years he had spent in Mexico after graduating from high school. He had written him two or three times a year and received answers, but another visit to Mexico had never again been mentioned. Langston had not written his father for several months now. He thought about doing it that evening but decided to put it off and go to bed instead. The next afternoon he received word that his father had died the previous evening—while Langston had been writing "Mailbox for the Dead."

Langston was quite sure his father had not left him or his mother anything in his will, but his father's sister in Indianapolis thought she might have inherited some money. She wired Langston $300 to go to Mexico to see about the will.

A few years earlier James Hughes had suffered a stroke. Ever since then he had lived with the three elderly, unmarried sisters whom he had known for thirty years and who had helped him when he had first arrived in Mexico. Langston would go to their house in Mexico City.

On arriving in Mexico City Langston found that he had been right not to expect to inherit anything from his father. He did not care. He had not liked his father and did not want his father's money or property. James Hughes had left everything to the three women, who were, according to Langston's later writings, the only people who had ever really liked his father. The aunt in Indianapolis was not mentioned in the will either. Though the three sisters were eager to share everything with Langston, he would take only enough of his father's bank deposits to repay his aunt the $300 he had spent coming there. After that, what was left would not even pay his return passage. So he stayed in Mexico until he could make enough money from his writings to go home.

Actually, Langston was delighted to have an excuse to stay in Mexico. He loved the Spanish language and greatly enjoyed the life style and customs of Latin America. He met a number of native and foreign artists, translated several Mexican short stories into English for publication in the United States, and went to bullfights every Sunday. It was a very pleasant winter. By spring he had sold a few stories. Then, with a young French photographer, Henri Cartier-Bresson, and a young Mexican poet, Andrés Henestrosa, he rented a flat. None of the three roommates had much money, but they shared what they had. He met several Mexicans who were as dark as American blacks, among them artist Miguel Covarrubias, and learned that there was African blood in many Mexicans. He also met some American blacks living in Mexico, some of whom had assimilated into Mexican society, where there was no color line.

But when Langston met a Cuban friend who had become a diplomat in Mexico, his peace was shattered. His friend immediately began to spread the word that a very important writer was in Mexico City. A round of interviews, sessions with photographers and artists, and requests to translate his poetry into Spanish made him decide that it was about time to think about going back to California.

When Langston returned to California in June, 1934, he learned that a friend of his, black writer Arna Bontemps, and his wife were in Los Angeles. He and Bontemps had written and published a children's story about Haiti, and they decided to do another. Bontemps was living with his wife and children in a cottage in the suburban black section of the city, and Langston moved in with them. Bontemps was unemployed, and Langston, as usual, did not have much money. But they shared what they had and managed to get by.

To supplement their income Langston would occasionally give poetry readings. However, because of his trip to Soviet Russia, he was now often plagued by censorship. Of course Langston was not communist. His visit to Russia and his favorable comments about it were enough, however, for many people to label him "red." One incident took place in Los Angeles, where he was scheduled to be one of several speakers in a program at the black YMCA. But it was rumored that he was communist, and the Y, wanting to avoid controversy, took his name off the program. But the Y's youth committee refused to drop Langston from the program. On the day of the program police tried to keep Langston out. Members of the youth committee told the audience why, and the entire audience moved to a place where Langston was allowed to speak.

After he and Bontemps finished the draft of their book, Langston settled again into Carmel-by-the-Sea for a good summer of writing. But soon after he arrived there he received word from his mother that she was ill and was staying with some distant cousins in Oberlin, Ohio. As usual, she had no money. Langston often marveled at his mother's ability to spend his money—on distant relatives, friends, anyone in need. He loved her kindheartedness

Arna Bontemps

but wished she were a little thriftier. He was disturbed by the tone of her letter, though, and as he had not seen her since his return from the Soviet Union, he decided to visit her. Besides, he had always wanted to see Oberlin. His grandmother had been the first black woman to attend Oberlin College, and it was there that she had married Sheridan Leary just before he went off to die fighting with John Brown.

When Langston arrived, he found his mother very ill with cancer. Although the doctor's fees were reasonable, it took nearly all Langston could earn to pay them. In order to make more money, Langston decided to try to sell some of his stories and articles in New York.

Almost as soon as he stepped out of the subway station into Harlem, he met an acquaintance who asked him if he was in New York to attend the rehearsals of his play. This was news to Langston. His play *Mulatto* had been in his agent's hands for five years, and this was the first he had heard of its even being sold. He visited his agent and signed the contracts. Then he went to see the rehearsals.

A number of changes had been made without consulting him, but as he watched the play he realized that the basic story was still intact. The changes had been made in order to make the play more "box office," and thus more profitable. It turned out to be a success indeed, running for more than a year on Broadway. And after leaving Broadway it traveled across the country for two more years, setting a record in America for number of performances of a play written by a black.

It was a comment on the times that neither Langston nor any of the black actors were invited to the white producer's party following the opening of the play. Langston even had a hard time collecting royalties and retaining sole authorship of his own play. Still, he was "hooked" on the theater, and from that year, 1935, on, he would devote much of his time to writing plays and establishing black theater groups. In the following years, he would almost single-handedly establish an authentic black national theater in Harlem, Chicago, Los Angeles, and elsewhere. In 1936, several of his plays were produced, among them, *Troubled Island, Little Ham,* and *When Little Jack Hollers* (which he wrote with Bontemps).

Meanwhile his mother had moved to Cleveland to be closer to her doctor. A letter was sent there from the Baltimore *Afro-American,* asking Langston to cover the activities of American blacks in Spain participating in the Spanish Civil War. Langston had always wanted to spend some time in Spain, but he was not sure he wanted to go there while the country was in the midst of civil war. Nevertheless he was short of money, and the *Afro-American* offered him four to six months in Spain at good pay. Two Cleveland newspapers also said they would pay for articles, so he quickly made preparations for the trip.

Langston paid his mother's rent for three months in advance, opened an account for her in the bank, and made out a will which he left in the bank. He hadn't much in the world, but he wanted to make sure that, if anything happened to him in Spain, any royalties earned from the sale of his books would go to his mother. As things turned out, of course, Langston returned from Spain unharmed. It was his mother who would die the following year.

The money Langston had provided to keep his family going was mysteriously gone, though, even before he left for Spain. It was not until he returned that he learned that his mother had used it to help out yet another distant cousin. Thus, even before he got to Spain, he had to send home most of his newspaper monies.

CHAPTER TWELVE

Langston traveled to Spain by way of Paris, where he saw many of the people whom he had known a dozen years before, when he was a doorman, a waiter, and a dishwasher in the Paris clubs. In fact, he almost wished he could stay in Paris with his friends, and radio reports of Fascist bombings of major Spanish cities did not help his mood.

As soon as the night train from Paris emerged from the long dark tunnel on the border between France and Spain, Langston knew he was in a country at war. Windows were shattered in the station building, holes made by machine gun bullets were visible in the walls of the customs house, and several bombed-out ruins of houses were nearby. Because of air raids, the trip to Barcelona took hours. Langston was so exhausted that he slept right through an air raid that night. But he did not sleep through the one the next night. A huge explosion actually lifted him clear off the bed. He sat in the hotel lobby with the other guests, listening to the bombs and the guns and the shattering windows, and his hands trembled. He had the worst stomach ache he had ever had in his life. Eventually he got used to the air raids, except for the eerie wail of the sirens sounding the air raid alert.

The war had begun in 1936, when army officers had attacked the Republican government in an attempt to overthrow it and set up a dictatorship. But the rebels had not counted on the resistance

Devastation in Madrid, Spain, from the Spanish Civil War

of the mass of common soldiers and common people. Soon the conflict had turned into a cruel and bloody civil war. On one side were the Loyalists, supporters of the old government, and on the other were the Fascists, led by General Franco and assisted by the air force and bombing power of dictators Hitler of Germany and Mussolini of Italy.

The war had inspired strong feeling throughout the rest of the world. Already hundreds of Americans in sympathy with the Loyalists had come to Spain to join the International Brigade as volunteer fighters. Other Americans—writers, artists, journalists, nurses—were also there, willing to help in any way they could.

Langston wanted to help, too, by using his writings to rally support for the Loyalists. Meanwhile, the American government, as well as the governments of England and France, refused to intervene. So while Germany and Italy supplied tanks, bombs, planes, and troops to the Fascists, the Loyalists were forced to rely on whatever unofficial help they could get.

For six months Langston lived close to the battlefronts of Spain, sharing in a small way the deprivation and hope of the common Spanish people. In Madrid, where he spent most of his time, food was scarce, for the enemy had succeeded in cutting off most of the city's food supply. Soon Langston knew every bar serving snacks with drinks and the times of day when they did so. Each day he would make the rounds trying to fill his stomach. As time went on, it got so bad that sometimes his hotel served nothing but bread soup with bread for dinner.

At least in Madrid he had always had a clean and comfortable bed to sleep in. This was not always the case nearer the battlefront. When Langston arrived in Albacete he found all the hotels packed and the only place to sleep a barracks on the outskirts of town. It was filled with wooden bunk beds, and when Langston arrived around midnight there was hardly an empty bunk. Finally, he found an unoccupied top bunk. Exhausted, he climbed up onto it, leaving all his clothes on, for it was a cold night. Hours later he was awakened from a deep sleep—and no wonder. His whole body was crawling with bedbugs! He considered killing them but knew there were too many. Anyway, he really didn't want squashed bedbugs all over his clothes. So, unable to do anything about it, he just went back to sleep.

During his trips up to the front lines Langston talked to many blacks from all parts of America serving in the International Brigade. The American battalions were named after Lincoln, Washington, and John Brown. There was no color line in the International Brigade. Blacks and whites served side by side, and whites served under black commanders. Blacks served in the medical units, too. Langston came upon two boys from Harlem driving ambulances to and from the front lines who should have been in high school back home.

Langston had been writing verses called "Letters from Spain." One, entitled "International Brigades, Lincoln Battalion, Somewhere in Spain, 1937," was about the irony of American blacks fighting against Moors (blacks from the Spanish colony of Morocco in Africa who had been forced to fight in the Fascist armies). The poem was in the form of a letter from an American black in the Brigades to a relative in the South:

Dear Brother at home:
We captured a wounded Moor today.
He was just as dark as me.
I said, Boy, what you doin' here,
Fightin' against the free?
He answered something in a language
I couldn't understand.
But somebody told me he was sayin'
They grabbed him in his land
And made him join the Fascist army
And come across to Spain
And he said he had a feelin'
He'd never get back home again.
He said he had a feelin'
The whole thing wasn't right.
He said he didn't know
These folks he had to fight.

Sometimes Langston read his poems to the black soldiers at the front. Although they liked the poems, the soldiers often asked why he had used slightly broken English and included grammatical mistakes. Most of the black Brigadeers were educated, they pointed out. But, Langston explained, many people who had little education, black and white, were fighting in Spain. Blacks, especially, had been forced into poorer schools or had been unable to go to school at all. He had used improper grammar in these poems to show that even Americans denied equal rights in their own country would fight to preserve a foreign government that would ensure these rights to its people.

Since he hadn't planned to stay into the winter months, Langston had not brought any warm clothes, and as the weather grew cold he was reminded that it was time to leave Spain. He had gotten his stories, stayed longer than the newspaper had agreed to pay him for, and seen just about all there was to see. With food so scarce he felt guilty eating the rations of those who could not leave. Nevertheless he felt sick at the thought of going. After a few final days in Valencia and Barcelona, he took the night train to Paris.

Langston arrived in Paris just in time for Christmas. He spent the day with some American friends, who fed him a wonderful home-cooked dinner. Paris was not as gay as it had been in the summer, for there was much talk of the war in Spain and fear it would spread. Many intellectuals believed Spain was just a training ground for Hitler and Mussolini in preparation for a coming worldwide war. Langston had wanted to spend the winter in France, but he had sent most of his money home to Cleveland and could not afford it. Anyway, his mother's illness worried him, and he decided he had better go straight home to see her.

Langston spent New Year's Eve, 1938, alone in Paris. "The year before, I had been in Cleveland," he later wrote. "The year before that in San Francisco. The year before that in Mexico City. The one before that at Carmel. And the year before Carmel in Tashkent. Where would I be when the next New Year came, I wondered?" [18] One thing he was sure of—he would still be making his living by writing. He had done so for nearly five years now, all the while traveling to new places and meeting new people and learning new things. During that time his interest in and involvement with only Harlem and the American black had broadened to include all the colored peoples of the world—in fact, all the people of the world.

The Last Years

CHAPTER THIRTEEN

Back once again in New York in January, 1938, Langston accepted an offer to set up a black theater in Harlem. By staging plays written by blacks and using black actors, black directors, and black scenic designers, the theater could help black people become skilled in the field. The second floor of an old building on West 125th Street served as the theater's home. It was called the Harlem Suitcase Theater, because all the equipment they had could have fit into one suitcase!

The first production of the Harlem Suitcase Theater opened on April 21. Tickets were only thirty-five cents, so Harlemites could afford them. Performances were given on weekends only, to make it easier for working people to attend. The play was one of Langston's, entitled *Don't You Want to Be Free?*; in it were included about a dozen of Langston's poems as well as many blues, spirituals, work chants, and jazz songs. No props or scenery were used, and the action took place right in the center of the theater, with the audience surrounding it. This was not an original idea. Langston had seen plays in Russia presented this way. He felt this arrangement increased the immediacy of the action and brought the audience closer not only to the actors but to the action as well. So when he had the opportunity to set up a theater in the United States he remembered the Russian method. In fact, he probably gave New York its first such "theater in the round." Artistic considerations aside, it was perfect for the small, impoverished theater company, which had little money for scenery or props anyway.

The play was a great success. When it was time for a new play to open, *Don't You Want to Be Free?* moved to another location in Harlem, and its total of 135 performances made it the longest-running play ever to be staged in Harlem.

In 1938 the country's economy, which had been steadily improving for some years, took another turn for the worse. As usual black people were hit hardest. Jobs were so scarce and rents so high that thousands of Harlem families were forced to live in damp, rat-infested basements, and the tuberculosis rate rose alarmingly. Feeling his people's despair, Langston threw himself into writing pamphlets and poems protesting the plight of blacks in America and injustice and inequality wherever it occurred.

Meanwhile he continued to do all he could to further the cause of the Spanish Loyalists and to win support for the Scottsboro boys who were still in jail. He wrote poems about attempts by Southern black sharecroppers to form a union. And he wrote about the poor blacks across America whose lives consisted of struggling constantly to survive in the face of grinding poverty and inequality. He had many of his poems printed in a cheap booklet entitled *A New Song* in order that people who could not afford books and who had never before read his poetry could do so now.

In early 1939 Langston traveled to Los Angeles to found the New Negro Theater, which also began its first season with *Don't You Want to Be Free?* Meanwhile he was at work on an autobiography, entitled *The Big Sea,* which would cover his growing-up years, and a film called *Way Down South,* his first work for Hollywood. He was, of course, pleased to have been invited to write a screenplay. But he was even more pleased about the Hollywood money he was being paid.

But Langston would not see much Hollywood money in his lifetime. While his being hired to write the screenplay for a black film represented a major breakthrough, it did not inaugurate any black Renaissance in Hollywood. Nearly forty years later it would still be rare for a Hollywood studio to hire a black writer.

In May Langston left Hollywood for Chicago, where he shut himself up in a hotel to finish his autobiography. But soon he was broke again and writing to his publisher for an advance on his uncompleted manuscript. He mailed the finished manuscript to New York by November, informing his editor that after his winter lecture tour he planned to start a second novel. But though he would mention it every couple of years after that, he never had enough money to just sit down and write it. He did write a second volume of his autobiography, calling it *I Wonder As I Wander*, and together the two books would recount his life all the way up to 1937. Written with a combination of sadness and humor that had characterized his life and his manner of looking at life, the books would be very well received by the critics.

It is unfortunate that Langston did not write an autobiography in his later years, for the two he wrote covered only his first thirty-five years, and as it turned out that was only about half his life. Certainly he did far less traveling abroad in his later life, but he did travel extensively in the United States. In fact, he seemed committed to a wandering life. "Six months in one place," he once told black writer Richard Wright, "is long enough to make one's life complicated." [19] He continued to meet famous people, learn more about human nature, and have many more valuable experiences from 1937 until his death, but he never chronicled them in his unique fashion, and the world is poorer for it.

The world and his native country in particular however, are much richer for the things he did do from 1937 on, such as establishing the small black theater groups. A third one he set up in Chicago in 1941, together with the others he had started, led to the formation of many such groups in other black communities across the country. These served, in many instances, as the only places where black playwrights could see their works performed and where black actors could get stage experience. Many of the country's most famous actors and playwrights got their start in these small community theater groups.

In the summer of 1942 Langston moved into a three-room

apartment in Harlem with the Harpers, two old friends of the family from Kansas who were like an adopted aunt and uncle. Harlem was in an increasingly restive and angry mood. The world war the Paris intellectuals had talked about when Langston was there had, of course, come about. German armies were advancing over Europe, and Japan had brought the United States into the war in 1941 with the bombing of Pearl Harbor. Americans called Hitler a racist and promised to destroy all his forces, all the while continuing its own racist practices at home. Blacks were often turned away from war industry plants that really needed workers. Some who attempted to join the armed services were rejected because of their race, or, if they were allowed to join, were given only the lowliest jobs.

This hypocrisy on the part of the United States deeply angered the black people. Yet they were aware of the seriousness of the German threat. If Hitler triumphed, all nonwhite peoples of the world would be in jeopardy. Langston had been too young to fight in World War I. He was now too old to fight in World War II. But he contributed to the war effort. In collaboration with various composers, he wrote the lyrics for songs in support of America and its fighting troops, which were broadcast on the radio and sung at freedom rallies. And, although he did not know it then, his writings were strengthening the resistance efforts of one of America's allies. Though Germany occupied Holland, the Dutch underground was extremely active. As part of its resistance movement, it secretly published some of Langston's writings in a booklet entitled *Lament for Dark Peoples and Other Poems*, and circulated it to show defiance of Nazi philosophy.

Although Langston and other black writers contributed in many ways to the U.S. war effort, they did not cease to use their writings to agitate for an end to discrimination, segregation, and other conditions that made life for blacks in America so hard. But at some point during the war years Langston began to examine his own work and the works of others, to see whether they were doing as much as they could for black people.

Most of what was written dealt with the pain and the suffering of black people. Langston realized this was too one-sided. "If the best of our writers continue to pour their talent into the tragedies of frustration and weakness, tomorrow will probably say, on the basis of available literary evidence, 'No wonder the Negroes never amounted to anything. There were no heroes among them. Defeat and panic, moaning, groaning, and weeping were their lot. Did nobody fight? Did nobody triumph?' "[20] From that time on, Langston devoted much of his writing to books and plays on black heroes and famous black people. Many of these books and plays were for children, because Langston thought black children were most in need of knowing about the glories and heroes of their race.

But Langston did not cease to write about the people he knew and loved best—the ordinary black people, whom he considered heroic in their own right. In 1942 he began writing about the one fictional character he would develop fully in his writing career. Until that time he had rarely written more than one poem or story about a single character. The closest he had come was with Madam Alberta K. Johnson. He'd written several poems about her, an archetypally strong, proud, and quick-witted black woman. One of them was, "Madam's Past History":

My name is Johnson—
Madam Alberta K.
The Madam stands for business.
I'm smart that way.

I had a
HAIR-DRESSING PARLOR
Before
The depression put
The prices lower.

Then I had a
BARBECUE STAND
Till I got mixed up
With a no-good man.

Cause I had a insurance
The WPA*
Said, We can't use you
Wealthy that way.

* The Works Progress Administration, the federal agency that created jobs for the unemployed during the 1930s.

I said
DON'T WORRY 'BOUT ME!
Just like the song,
You WPA folks take care of yourself—
And I'll get along.

I do cooking
Day's work, too!
Alberta K. Johnson—
Madam to you.

But Langston never developed Madam Alberta K. Johnson the way he would Jesse B. Semple, better known as "Simple." The idea of Simple as a character came to Langston one evening in 1942 while he was relaxing in a bar near his apartment on St. Nicholas Avenue. Nearby, a young man was telling his girl friend about his job—making cranks in a New Jersey war materials factory. Casually, Langston leaned over and asked what the function was of the cranks, whereupon the man answered, "How do I know what them cranks crank? You know white folks don't tell Negroes what cranks crank." Langston thought that was a refreshingly direct answer. Intrigued by his new acquaintance, he spent hours in the bar that evening, and many other evenings, talking to him. What resulted, in 1943, was Langston's first book of "Simple" stories, a collection of conversations between a well-educated writer (probably Langston himself) and an uneducated, hard-working Harlemite. Through Simple, Langston seemed to have found a type of character he felt was needed in black literature. For though Simple has more troubles than can be imagined, there is nothing defeated about him. In fact his troubles have brought him a special kind of wisdom.

Simple was not patterned after just one man. He was intended to symbolize the black race, indeed the poor and downtrodden of every race—subjected to pain and suffering and yet coming through it with a sort of humorous wisdom. One of the most popular passages from Simple is the following, about feet:

"These feet have stood on every rock from the Rock of Ages to 135th and Lenox. These feet have supported everything from a cotton bale to a hungry woman. These feet have walked ten thousand miles working for white folks and another ten thou-

> *sand keeping up with colored. These feet have stood at altars, crap tables, free lunches, bars, graves, kitchen doors, betting windows, hospital clinics, WPA desks, social security railings, and in all kinds of lines from soup lines to the draft. If I just had four feet, I could have stood in more places longer. As it is, I done wore out seven hundred pairs of shoes, eighty-nine tennis shoes, twelve summer sandals, also six loafers. The socks that these feet have bought could build a knitting mill. The corns I've cut away would dull a German razor. The bunions I forgot would make you ache from now till Judgment Day. If anybody was to write the history of my life, they should start with my feet."* [21]

At the time he created Simple, Langston was writing a weekly column for the black newspaper, *The Chicago Defender.* He decided to include in it some of the Simple stories. The first column devoted to Simple appeared in 1943, and it was an immediate success. Later, Langston would also do a column for the *New York Post,* and Simple would appear frequently there as well. Some people criticized Langston for writing so many Simple stories. They claimed Simple was not real, that he did not ring true. However, many other people did not agree, among them one reader from Tennessee. Once, after a story appeared mentioning that Simple liked possum meat, that reader sent Simple a possum, neatly packed in ice, all the way from Tennessee!

Some people objected to the humor in Simple, saying that being black in America was not a laughing matter. But Langston knew that one of the black people's greatest strengths was their ability to laugh. He understood, too, that humor can be a powerful weapon against injustice and cruelty.

Through the success of his Simple stories, Langston realized his high school dream that people all over the world would read his stories. The five Simple books have been translated into many languages and are loved by people of many lands. For them, Simple is a kind of Everyman, and his message is universal. In fact, though Langston is known primarily as a poet, many critics believe Simple to be his greatest contribution to American literature.

CHAPTER FOURTEEN

Throughout the 1940s Langston continued his yearly speaking and poetry reading tours of the country—he needed the money. Unfortunately he had never had a bestseller or any other stroke of financial luck. Though his books for children sold quite well, his major works did not. *The Weary Blues,* his first book of poems, sold only seven thousand copies over twenty-five years. *Fine Clothes to the Jew,* his second volume, did so poorly that the plates for it were melted down during his publisher's drive to economize during World War II. His poems written during the war years did equally poorly. This is not unusual for books of poetry, for Americans just do not buy them in large numbers. But biographies and autobiographies usually do sell well, and so it was surprising that Langston's autobiographies did not. (*The Big Sea,* for example, sold only five thousand copies in its first ten years.) Thus Langston, never able to live on the royalties from his books, was forced to rely on money earned from articles, newspaper columns, and so on, to keep a roof over his head and food in his stomach.

Aside from the money he earned, taking his poetry directly to people had always been important for Langston. He spoke at colleges and high schools, trying to instill racial pride in black students and help explain the feelings of black people to white students. During the war years he told of the heroic deeds of black soldiers, sometimes voicing the hope that perhaps the war would cause people to be more decent to each other. During those years Langston experienced a sizable amount of *in*decency, for anti-communism was growing in the United States, and anyone who had been to Soviet Russia was suspect. To be black in America was bad enough, but Langston was a black man who had visited Soviet Russia and, even worse, had reported favorable things about it. All this let him in for more than his share of anti-communist flack.

However it did not take long for Langston to understand what was *really* behind the cries of "red," for those who cried loudest were also the strongest supporters of segregation. Racism can take a variety of forms; labeling someone a communist had become a convenient way of masking racist hatred. Nevertheless, for many people the "red" label became attached to Langston. Places where he was to appear were picketed, and though he often remarked that being picketed must mean he had something worthwhile to say, sometimes it did place him in uncomfortable positions.

Once, in Gary, Indiana, a group of black teachers faced the possibility of losing their jobs if Langston spoke at one of the public schools. Another time in a different city, the parents of some students at a white high school protested Langston's coming so loudly that the principal asked for clearance from the FBI, who, since Langston did end up speaking there, apparently assured him that Langston was not communist. However, as extra insurance, the school authorities invited all the town's black ministers and respectable black leaders to sit on the stage as further proof of his respectability. Langston chuckled wryly as he thought of what must be going through the minds of the white students. Never before had they seen even one black on their auditorium stage. Now suddenly they were confronted with an entire delegation!

In the 1950s things got even worse. Waves of what some called "know-nothing patriotism" swept the country. Basically, this was a movement founded on the idea that the United States was right, no matter what, and that anyone who questioned anything about the United States was anti-American. Anti-communist sentiment ran high. People in government or in the public eye who at any time in the past had questioned their country were viewed suspiciously or considered to have "communist tendencies." The most energetic communist hunter was Senator Joseph McCarthy. He dominated Washington and newspaper headlines with his accusations against so-called communists. With the support of congressional investigating committees he summoned well-known people from all fields to testify to their patriotism or defend themselves against accusations that they were communists.

Langston was called before the McCarthy committee in March, 1953, when the senator was trying to embarrass a government agency by accusing it of buying radical books for overseas libraries. Langston testified that he was not and never had been a communist and that he believed in a democratic solution to social and economic problems. (Langston had always been non-political; he felt that any problem could be solved if people would just work together instead of against each other. But he did not say this at the committee hearings.) When asked to name people he knew who were communists, he would not. He was finally dismissed.

In those times, however, merely the fact that one had been called to testify amounted, in the public mind, to conviction. Langston's involvement with the committee was not forgotten, especially by those people who did not like him or what he stood for. For a long time he received few invitations to lecture, which meant that an important source of income was lost. Though eventually the invitations began to come again, his appearances were often accompanied by picketing. Even long after McCarthy was exposed as a self-server and fanatic, the damage he had done remained. Not until the civil rights upheavals of the 1960s did the country, in its concern over new black militancy, begin to forget.

By the 1960s many black people who had tried to work nonviolently for equal rights and an end to discrimination had begun to question their methods. Young blacks, especially, were tired of quietly taking beatings and verbal abuse. It seemed whites would never accept integration. In reaction many blacks decided they did not want it either. All they wanted was equality, and some were prepared to use any measures to get it. Antiwhite feeling grew strong in American black communities. The call was no longer for integration but for separation.

Langston testifying before the Senate Investigating Subcommittee, March, 1953

It was the time of the Black Power movement. Much that had previously been acceptable to blacks was acceptable no longer. After twenty-five years Langston stopped writing Simple stories. "The racial climate has gotten so complicated and bitter that cheerful and ironic humor is less and less understandable to so many people," he explained sadly.[22]

Langston had always been a gentle man, a man who would often become physically ill when angry or upset. But in the sixties his writings became angrier and more defiant. One of his more well-known poems, written during this period, was recorded by the singer Nina Simone. The poem was written the year Langston died.

THE BACKLASH BLUES

Mister Backlash, Mister Backlash,
Just who do you think I am?
Tell me, Mister Backlash,
Who do you think I am?,
You raise my taxes, freeze my wages,
Send my son to Vietnam.

You give me second-class houses,
Give me second-class schools,
Second-class houses
And second-class schools.
You must think us colored folks
Are second-class fools.

When I try to find a job
To earn a little cash,
Try to find myself a job
To earn a little cash,
All you got to offer
Is a white backlash.

interpretation is largely opinion, so I choose to value my own.

But the world is big,
The world is big and round,
Great big world, Mister Backlash,
Big and bright and round—
And it's full of folks like me who are
Black, Yellow, Beige, and Brown.

Mister Backlash, Mister Backlash,
What do you think I got to lose?
Tell me, Mister Backlash,
What you think I got to lose?
I'm gonna leave you, Mister Backlash,
Singing your mean old backlash blues.

You're the one,
Yes, you're the one
Will have the blues.

Some have said that these writings may have been an attempt to prove to the militant black younger generation that he still had something important to say. But it is probably closer to the truth to say that Langston was angry and frustrated too, and only now did the climate allow such open expression of anger. Nor were they his first angry poems. In fact, one of his angriest, "Christ in Alabama," had been written in the early 1930s.

Langston's most militant book of poems, *The Panther and the Lash,* published in 1967, sold phenomenally well for a book of poetry, proving that the younger generation believed his ideas still valid. Sadly, Langston was denied the enjoyment of its success, for he died two months before it was published.

Throughout the final years of his life, Langston continued to be as prolific and productive as ever. The Harpers had died some years earlier, and he had moved into a narrow, three-story brownstone at No. 20 West 127th Street. His workroom on the top floor was a clutter of books, manuscripts, letters, and magazines. He liked nothing better than to have five or six projects in the works at once. He became so engrossed in his work that he deliberately arranged his day to allow for the least possible number of interruptions while working. Sounds from the busy street below sometimes bothered him, as did the telephone. So he would work from midnight until dawn, and then sleep from dawn to early afternoon. Then, his working and sleeping accomplished, he would be ready for the day's interruptions.

Often he took afternoon walks, or, during the season, worked on his garden beside his stoop. Milton Meltzer, who had worked with Langston on two anthologies and had begun a biography of him during this period, recalls that Langston's garden hardly covered a square yard. The first year he planted it, the neighborhood children had stepped all over the plants and ruined his garden. The next year Langston invited the children to help him plant. They each put their name on stakes to identify where their particular plants would grow. Needless to say, the garden grew undisturbed that year.

Langston liked young people and took an active interest in them. In his last years he did much to help young writers get started. He was always sending their material to his publishers and would often recommend them for projects or articles he could have handled. He also could have used the money he would have been paid for doing them. But he remembered how hard it had been for him to reach the point where he could make a living by writing, and he understood how important that little extra push was. And there was no generation gap between Langston and the young writers; they spoke freely to one another, and their differences of opinion were never caused by differences in age.

There was an ageless quality about Langston Hughes, which made it seem he would somehow endure forever. But he died on May 22, 1967, at the age of sixty-five, due to prolonged heart and kidney trouble. Many people simply could not believe he was gone. A memorial service was held a few days later in Harlem. Hundreds of his friends attended. It was not really a sad occasion, for Langston was the sort of man who remained so vividly in one's memory that it seemed almost as if he were still alive. Nor would he have wanted his friends to be sad. He even made sure that humor—his tried and true weapon against sadness—played a part in his memorial service by arranging for someone to read his poem "Wake":

Tell all my mourners
To mourn in red—
Cause there ain't no sense
In my bein' dead.

And at the end of the service, a request he had made before he died was carried out. As a parting joke to his friends, a jazz trio played the old tune, "Do Nothing Till You Hear from Me."

Notes

1. Richard Ellmann and Robert O'Clair, eds., *The Norton Anthology of Modern Poetry* (New York: W. W. Norton & Company, Inc., 1973), p. 634.

2. Langston Hughes, *The Big Sea* (New York and London: Alfred A. Knopf, 1945; also, New York: Hill and Wang, 1963), p. 14.

3. *Ibid.*, p. 26.

4. *Ibid.*, p. 17.

5. *Ibid.*, p. 18.

6. *Ibid.*, p. 24.

7. *Ibid.*, p. 47.

8. *Ibid.*, p. 54.

9. *Ibid.*, p. 81.

10. *Ibid.*, p. 89.

11. *Ibid.*, pp. 97–98.

12. *Ibid.*, p. 209.

13. *Ibid.*, pp. 267–268.

14. *Ibid.*, p. 308.

15. *Ibid.*, p. 228.

16. *Ibid.*, p. 317.

17. Langston Hughes, *I Wonder As I Wander* (New York: Hill and Wang, 1956), p. 114.

18. *Ibid.*, p. 405.

19. Milton Meltzer, *Langston Hughes: A Biography* (New York: Thomas Y. Crowell Co., Inc., 1968), p. 228.

20. *Ibid.*, pp. 226–227.

21. Langston Hughes, "Feet Live Their Own Life," *The Best of Simple* (New York: Hill and Wang, 1961), pp. 2–3.

22. Meltzer, p. 248.

Bibliography

Bone, Robert A. *The Negro Novel in America.* New Haven, Conn.: Yale University Press, 1958; rev. ed., 1965.

Braithwaite, William S. "The Negro in Literature." *Crisis* XXVIII (Sept., 1924), 204–210.

Calverton, V. F. "The Advance of Negro Literature." *Opportunity* IV (Feb., 1926), 54–55.

Davis, Arthur P. "Jesse B. Semple: Negro American." *Phylon* XV (Spring, 1954), 21–28.

Dickinson, Donald. *A Bio-Bibliography of Langston Hughes.* Hamden, Conn.: Shoe String Press, 1967; 2nd ed., 1972.

Ellmann, Richard, and Robert O'Clair, eds. *The Norton Anthology of Modern Poetry.* New York: W. W. Norton & Co., Inc., 1973, 633ff.

Emanuel, James A. *Langston Hughes.* New York: Twayne Publishers, 1967.

Emanuel, James A., and Theodore L. Gross, eds., *Dark Symphony: Negro Literature in America.* New York: The Free Press, 1968, 205–208.

Gloster, Hugh M. *Negro Voices in American Fiction.* Chapel Hill: University of North Carolina Press, 1948; New York: Russell & Russell, 1965.

Hughes, Langston. *The Best of Simple.* New York: Hill and Wang, 1961.

———. *The Big Sea.* New York and London: Alfred A. Knopf, Inc., 1945; New York: Hill and Wang, 1963.

———. *The Dream Keeper.* New York: Alfred A. Knopf, Inc., 1932.

———. *I Wonder As I Wander.* New York: Hill and Wang, 1956.

———. *The Panther and the Lash.* New York: Alfred A. Knopf, Inc., 1967.

Littlejohn, David. *Black on White: A Critical Survey of Writing by American Negroes.* New York: Grossman Publishing Co., 1965.

Meltzer, Milton. *Langston Hughes: A Biography.* New York: Thomas Y. Crowell Co., Inc., 1968.

Ottley, Roi. *New World A-Coming: Inside Black America.* Boston: Houghton Mifflin Co., 1943.

Presley, James. "The American Dream of Langston Hughes." *Southwest Review* XLVIII (Autumn, 1963), 380–386.

Randolph, Richard. *The Negro Vanguard.* New York: Holt, Rinehart & Winston, 1959.

"Special Langston Hughes Number." *CLA Journal* XI, 4 (June, 1968).

"Special Supplement on Langston Hughes." *Freedomways* VIII, 2 (Spring, 1968).

Van Doren, Carl. "Negro Renaissance." *Century* CXI (March, 1926), 635–637.

Index

About the Author

Jim Haskins, writer, teacher, lecturer, and widely published author, has degrees from Georgetown University, Alabama State University, and the University of New Mexico. He is currently associate professor in the Experimental College at Staten Island Community College, New York City. He is also a visiting lecturer at the Graduate School of Education at Manhattanville College, Purchase, New York, and, during summers, a visiting lecturer in Folklore and Literature at Indiana University–Purdue University, Indianapolis.

Mr. Haskins is author of some twenty-four books for adult and juvenile audiences. His adult books include the highly acclaimed *Diary of a Harlem Schoolteacher, Pinckney Benton Stewart Pinchback, The Psychology of Black Language* (co-author), and *Black Manifesto for Education* (editor). Among his juvenile titles are *From Lew Alcindor to Kareem Abdul Jabbar; Witchcraft, Mysticism and Magic in the Black World; Street Gangs: Yesterday and Today; The Creoles of Color of New Orleans,* and, for Franklin Watts, *The Consumer Movement* and *The Picture Life of Malcolm* X.